Build Your Own
Web Site

About the Author

David Karlins is a freelance web designer, an author, and a teacher. Hundreds of thousands of readers around the world have used David's books on Dreamweaver, FrontPage, and graphic design software to create their own web sites.

Build Your Own Web Site

David Karlins

McGraw-Hill/Osborne

New York   Chicago   San Francisco   Lisbon   London   Madrid   Mexico City
Milan   New Delhi   San Juan   Seoul   Singapore   Sydney   Toronto

The McGraw·Hill Companies

McGraw-Hill/Osborne
2100 Powell Street, Floor 10
Emeryville, California 94608
U.S.A.

To arrange bulk purchase discounts for sales promotions, premiums, or fund-raisers, please contact **McGraw-Hill/**Osborne at the above address. For information on translations or book distributors outside the U.S.A., please see the International Contact Information page immediately following the index of this book.

Build Your Own Web Site

1234567890 QPD QPD 019876543

ISBN 0-07-222953-5

Publisher
Brandon A. Nordin

Vice President & Associate Publisher
Scott Rogers

Acquisitions Editor
Marjorie McAneny

Project Editor
Mark Karmendy

Acquisitions Coordinator
Tana Allen

Technical Editor
David Elderbrock

Copy Editor
Lisa Theobald

Proofreader
Susie Elkind

Indexer
Rebecca Plunkett

Computer Designers
Lucie Ericksen, Tabitha M. Cagan

Illustrators
Melinda Moore Lytle, Michael Mueller, Lyssa Wald

Series Design
Jean Butterfield

Cover Series Design and Cover Illustration
Ted Holladay

This book was composed with Corel VENTURA™ Publisher.

To nonfiction.

Contents

Part I
Preparing to Build Your Web Site

Part III
Keeping Your Web Site Working and Up to Date

Acknowledgments

This book benefited from the contributions of an extraordinary group of reviewers including web designers, teachers, and folks who used the "beta" version of the book to build their own web sites. I really appreciate the time and energy each of you put into providing very useful feedback!

I was able to draw on the expert insights of David Elderbrock, who stepped down from his perch as a leading expert on web functionality to serve as technical editor for this book. And thanks to all the editors at Osborne, especially Margie McAneny who shared my vision for this book and brought it to life.

Introduction

You have in your hands a rather unique book. Rather than starting from how to use this or that particular graphic or web design software tool, this book tells you exactly *how to build a web site*!

Over the course of years of writing, teaching, and designing sites myself, I've always felt a tremendous need for a book that covers the entire scope of building a web site in a concentrated way. As one of my students put it, "most web design books start assuming you know something you don't, and end leaving you up in the air on where to go next." This book starts from square one—you sitting at your computer—and takes you through the entire process of creating, publishing, and promoting your site.

Obviously a book of this scope cannot provide the same kind of depth that a bookshelf full of books on graphic design, usability, bandwidth, and so on can provide. So, in the course of this book, I'll point you to my favorite resources for a more full exploration of various features of creating a web site.

You might develop your web design skills to the level where you'll have your own bookshelf full of resource books. Or, this book might be all the web design information you'll ever need. In either case, you can sit down with this book at your computer and create a web site right now, with no additional resources.

Who Is This Book For?

I originally intended this book to be a resource for beginners—people who need a web site for their small business, their school or class, their club, their non-profit, their artwork, their family, their soccer team, or their poetry. However, when I asked many of my colleagues to review the book, I learned something interesting—veteran and skilled professional web designers were finding this book essential as well.

Actually, I'm not surprised by that. You can read all the books you want on Dreamweaver, FrontPage, and Photoshop, but they don't help you decide what kind of server space to purchase. You can study Jacob Nielson's books on web page usability and Vincent Flanders' funny books about web pages that "suck" (and how to avoid them—and you should), but those books won't help you figure out what CGI scripts are and how you can use them without learning to write Perl programs. In short, there are just so many gaps and holes in most folks' understanding of the process of creating a web site that I really think this book will be valuable for both beginners and experienced graphic and web designers.

What Do You Need to Build a Web Site?

You need three things to build your own web site: this book, a computer, and an internet connection. That's it. If you're starting from scratch, on a bare-bones budget, and want to get a web site up quickly with almost no expense, this book will show you how to do that utilizing the free, downloadable web page tools that come with Yahoo! GeoCities web sites.

If you elect to use one of the two web design software packages that dominate the market—Dreamweaver or FrontPage—this book will show you how to create a more complex web site. I've written nine FrontPage and Dreamweaver books, and I've taught thousands of students to use those programs in my live and online classes. Based on that experience, I've distilled the basic steps to create an effective and attractive Dreamweaver or FrontPage site into compact chapters in this book.

In general, throughout this book, I take a kind of "two-tier" approach to web design, graphic, media, animation, and scripting tools. I'll show you, for example, how to prepare an image for the Web in the free Paint program that comes with Microsoft Windows, *or* in Adobe Photoshop.

This book is compact and starts with the basics. That does not mean that the web site you create using this book will be simple or crude. You will learn to include digital audio and video, and animate your site and connect it to server-based databases to manage mailing lists and guestbooks.

If you're new to building a web site, I wouldn't invest in any additional software until you read this book. As you work your way through the chapters, you'll be able to make informed and careful decisions on what kind of software you need now, what you might use later, and what you don't need at all.

How to Use This Book

One way to use this book is to start at Chapter 1 and work your way through the book to Chapter 9. I organized the material in a way that I thought many web designers, especially beginners, would find it helpful. Exactly because so many of us have gaps in our understanding of the process of building a web site, I think many of you will find it worthwhile to read through the book from beginning to end (we tried to keep it short!) before you even start to create a web site.

That said, you can also jump around in this book all you want. If you've got a domain name, feel free to skip to buying server space. If you've got your images all prepared as web-ready JPEGs, skim through that section and move right into designing your pages.

Part I of this book might be the most valuable. Many of the folks I asked to review this book in advance have commented that if they knew then what they know now (after reading Chapters 1–3) they could have saved themselves an incredible amount of time and stress. Chapter 1 alerts you to what you need to have in place before you create a web site, and it includes a number of warnings that will keep you from trekking too far down dead ends. Chapter 1 explains how to organize the whole process of building your site. I've created hundreds of web sites, and I'll share some approaches and methods that will make the process much more fun and rewarding. Plus, I'll evaluate FrontPage, Dreamweaver, and other web design tools, and help you select the best software for you needs.

Chapter 2 sorts out the technical stuff. How do you get a domain name? What is server space? What is bandwidth? And how much of what do you need? Read Chapter 2 before you waste time and money on a site that won't work for you.

In Chapter 3, I explain how to pull together all the content you'll need for your web site. You need text and images, and I'll explain how to prepare images for the web, whether you're comfortable with Photoshop or relying on the free software that comes with your computer or scanner. I'll also show you quick, easy ways to prepare audio and video files for the web, how to create PDF files for your site, and how to use Flash files in your web pages.

Part II of the book is divided into four chapters—one each on GeoCities' PageBuilder, Macromedia Dreamweaver, and Microsoft FrontPage, and one on promoting your site. If you're trying to decide what software is best for your site, I suggest you read through Chapters 4–6. Later, after you pick a web design program, return to the appropriate chapter for step-by-step detailed instructions. If you're already committed to FrontPage or Dreamweaver, skip to those chapters. I've boiled down the content to the things you *really need* to create an attractive, usable site. Chapter 7 shows you how to collect data from visitors in forms, connect to server scripts that manage e-mail lists, create search indexes, and informs you about other essential *server-based* web page features. I've found several free, online server resources that you can use, and you'll be able to apply the techniques I show you to connecting to any CGI script at any server.

Finally, Part III of this book shows you how to promote and maintain your site. Chapter 8 demystifies how search engines find and list your site, and explains how to get listed and improve your listings at Yahoo!, Google, and other popular search sites. The troubleshooting advice in Chapter 9 is gleaned from years of e-mails from frustrated students, clients, and readers. I've compiled problem-solving tips that will calm you down and lead you past those bumps in the road that every web designer encounters in publishing a web site—especially wrestling with annoying upload issues.

Tools, Tips, and Heads Up!

Sprinkled liberally throughout this book, between the steps and the images, are boxes with Tips of the Trade, or "Heads Up" warnings. I've used the Tips of the Trade callouts to share some candid insights, advice, or opinions that will spare you frustration as you follow the steps on that page. Take the "Heads Up" warnings as cautionary notes that steer you around mistakes that can blow your site, trash your images, or wipe out your files! Each chapter begins with a "Tools of the Trade" section that provides a list of software needed for that particular chapter.

A Companion Web Site for This Book

It's only fitting that a book about creating web sites *should have a web site*. I've created a companion web site for this book at www.buildyourownwebsite.us.

The web site supplements the book with additional resources, tools, and links. I'll use the web site to provide timely updates to book content as needed, and—from time to time—to address issues raised by readers. *You can use the book's web site* to interact with other readers as well as with me.

As you read this book, and after you finish, please feel free to drop in at the book's web site to keep me posted on how things are going, as well as to connect with others who are building their own web sites. I'll "see" you at www.buildyourownwebsite.us!

Part I

Preparing to Build Your Web Site

Chapter 1

Before You Get Started

What exactly *is* a web site? To use an analogy, a web site is like a house. A house requires a physical space (a lot), a structure (the walls, floors, and so on), furnishings, and for anyone to be able to find your house, it needs an address. Building a house would be chaos without a blueprint, so before you begin to build, you need to come up with a plan that reflects the way you want your house to look.

Similarly, four basic elements are involved in planning and creating a web site:

❏ You need some kind of plan (often in flowchart format) before you start to put your web site together, along with some design ideas (such as a color scheme) that can be jotted down in a notebook.

❏ You need a *space* to store your site content, where visitors from around the world can find it. This space is your *web server*—typically a powerful and highly reliable computer with special software that enables it to share information over the Internet.

❏ You need *content* for your web site. Your site content is the text, images, and media files you share in your web pages, along with the special coding required to display this content in an attractive format on your web page.

❏ Finally, nobody will be able to use your web site without a web *address*, which is called a Uniform Resource Locator (URL). This address allows people to find your site on the Internet. It is usually in the form *http://www.buildyourownwebsite.info*, comprising the usual *http://www*, plus a *domain name*, such as *buildyourownwebsite.us*, that is easy for people to remember.

What You'll Need for Your Web Site

This chapter outlines the process of designing a site, collecting site content, purchasing a domain name, and contracting for server space.

The four main phases of creating your web site do not have to occur in any particular order. You might, for example, first purchase a domain name, and then contract for web server space, and then design your site. Or you might design your site (using your own home or office computer) and later contract for a domain name and server space.

Designing Your Site

The single most important question to answer when you design your web site is What's the point? What information are you trying to convey? If you are selling services or a product, what is the most important thing about your product or service that visitors should find at your web site? If you are providing information, what is the most important piece of information you want to share, and what are secondary points you want to communicate? As you sit down to chart out your web site, start by making a list of the following:

❏ The *most important* thing at the web site

❏ Five to seven other important things at the web site

❏ The *audience* for your site (be specific—their age? Cultural background? Reading level? Attention span?)

For more help in sorting out the theme of your site, see the article "Develop Your Web Strategy" at this book's web site, *www.buildyourownwebsite.us*.

Folks new to web design often confuse or combine the process of *site* design with the task of *page* design. Page design refers to the way text, images, and other objects (such as media) are laid out on your page. But to create a usable site, you'll first want to have a basic idea of how your *entire* site (all your pages together) will be available to visitors.

Your *home page* is the page visitors will see when they first come to your site. You can think of your home page as the lobby in an office building or the living room in your home. You will want to show some *essential* information at your home page, but more importantly, you'll want to show *links* (clickable text or images) that allow visitors to get to the rest of the content at your site. The entire system of links in your site is sometimes called a web site *navigation flow*.

The most important part of your site to plan in advance is the navigation flow. Ask yourself the following questions: What links should be available at your home page? What pages should visitors be able to access from what other pages? Professional web designers start by creating flowcharts, such as the one shown in Figure 1-1, that identify how visitors will move around within a site.

Figure I-I
This flowchart includes a rough mockup of the site home page and uses lines and arrows to indicate navigation options from each page to other pages.

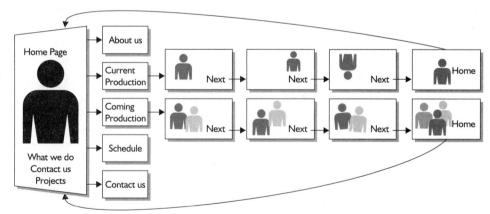

In addition to designing a navigation flow, you'll want to plan a coherent (consistent) and aesthetic (good-looking) look and feel for your site.

Choose a background page color and a standard text color to use for all your pages. In addition, you might design or locate artwork that can be used for logos identifying your site, as well as clickable navigation icons.

Colors that are reliably supported by a wide variety of computers (PCs, Macs, and others) as well as most browsers are called *web-safe colors*—there are 216 of these colors. If you use colors that aren't web-safe, your visitor's web browser might substitute a color that's *different* from the one you selected. Restrict yourself to web-safe colors when you plan a color scheme for your web site.

Two naming systems are used for web-safe colors: RGB (values for a mixture of red, blue, green), and the hexadecimal system (a combination of six letters or numbers that identify combinations of red, blue, and green). Lynda Weinman is the acknowledged guru of web color schemes. Her site, *www.lynda.com*, has helpful web color ideas and resources. You can find a list of web-safe colors, along with their hexadecimal and RBG names, at *www.lynda.com/hexh.html*.

The best way to get your creative juices flowing is to visit and study similar or competing web sites. Note the approaches these sites take to navigation: What links are available at the home page? How are links laid out on the home page?

Print pages you like, and keep them handy as models when you design your own site. Bookmark pages you want to emulate, so you can return to them later for ideas and inspiration. Note the colors used in the sites you like, the design of the pages, the use of images, and what kinds of navigation (link) options are available to visitors.

For more background on designing your site, see the article "Design and Create Your Site" at this book's web site, *www.buildyourownwebsite.us*.

Now that you have a basic idea of what's involved in building a web site, you're ready to take the next steps. Regardless of which tool you use to create your web site—PageBuilder, FrontPage, or Dreamweaver—you will need to have a domain name and a web server before you can upload your site to the Internet. You'll also need to have your files in web-friendly formats.

Collecting Site Content

In Chapter 3, you'll learn to prepare text, image, and media files for your web site. But even before you begin to do that, you'll want to start collecting the content that you want to include in your site. If you already have digital files with the text, images, and media you plan to include in your web site, that's great! All you need to do is organize them into folders on your computer, or on a CD, so you'll be able to access them quickly when you need them (see Figure 1-2).

Figure I-2
Web site files
assembled in a
folder include
Word documents,
images, audio,
and video files.

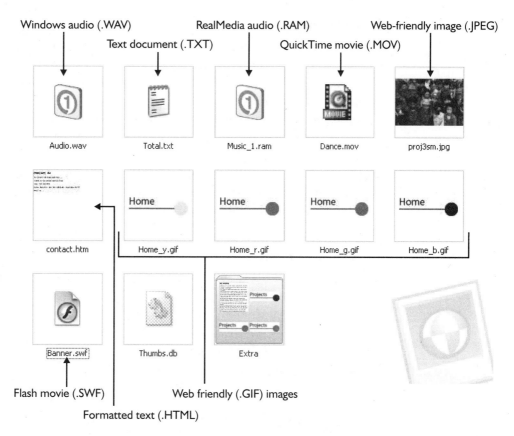

If, for example, you will be adapting files from a printed brochure, newsletter, catalog, or newsletter for your web site, arrange with the designer or desktop publisher to provide you with those files. If someone developed music or video that you want to include in your site, ask whether that music or video is available in a digital format (on CD, for example).

If your text files are scribbled on a scratch pad, your images are photos, and your video is on a VHS tape, that's OK, too. You'll simply need to do some typing, scanning, and converting to make this content digitized and available for the web. Chapter 3 will walk you through the steps necessary to transform this content into web-friendly formatting. But it's *still* a good idea to *collect* all this content—in a file folder or envelope—so that it's handy and accessible when you create your web site.

Securing Server Space

In almost every case, you won't buy and configure your own web server. That requires a powerful computer, an expensive and very fast Internet connection, 24/7 maintenance, and a lot of expertise at configuring the complex software that enables a server to function.

You'll probably rent server space from one of the thousands of commercial firms that provide space for web sites ranging from a few pages to huge commercial sites. The cost of reliable web hosting for a small web site can be as low as five dollars a month. Sites that present more content, and get more visitors, cost more. Chapter 2 itemizes the features you should look for in selecting a web site provider, along with detailed shopping tips.

What's in a Domain Name?

A domain name is the text a visitor enters in the address bar in his or her browser to find your web site. A catchy, easy-to-remember domain name can be very useful. Companies that sell domain names will help you search for an available name closest to the one you want. They might suggest a similar name to the one you are looking for (for example, *i-shoes.com* instead of *shoes.com*, as shown in Figure 1-3). Or they might suggest you try an alternative domain name extension. For instance, if you wanted *shoestore.com*, a domain name seller might suggest *shoes.us*.

Figure 1-3
Hunting for available domain names at register.com

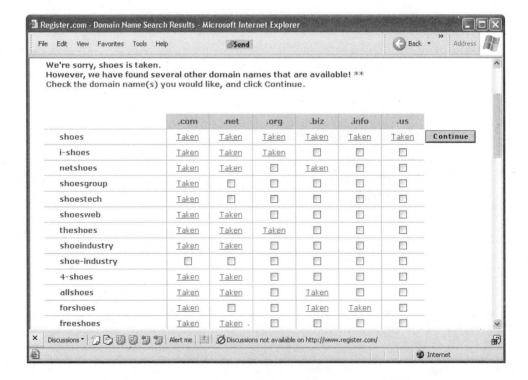

A domain name extension is the part of the domain name that comes after the "dot." Every country has its own (Canada is *.ca*, Australia is *.au*, and so on). In addition to extensions associated with countries, other domain name extensions are associated with different types of sites. The *.gov* extension is used for government agencies, *.com* or *.co* for commercial sites, and *.edu* for educational sites. The *.org* extension is often associated with nonprofit organizations, *.net* with network services, and the *.info* extension is used for sites that provide information. A good site for information on domain name extensions is *www.igoldrush.com/alt_ext.htm*.

Under the Hood—What Is in a Web Site

Web pages can include text, images, and media. Beyond that, web pages use HTML, HyperText Markup (formatting) Language, to format and present this content. Other tools, such as the JavaScript programming language, is used to make elements on your page (such as images) change and move around. For the most part, you won't need to worry much about how HTML formats your web page background color blue or how JavaScript makes your image change when a visitor clicks on it. All three web site software tools covered in this book generate HTML and JavaScript along with other coding behind the scenes, while you design your page in a *WYSIWYG* (What You See Is What You Get) design view.

In preparing to build your web site, you need to consider what kind of content you want on your site. The most basic web sites have formatted text and images as well. You can also include animation, interactivity, and media files on your site.

The most frequently used elements in web pages are listed in Table 1-1.

Type of File/ Filename Extension	What It Does	Where It Comes From
HTML: HTML, HTM, XHTML	HTML controls page design and text formatting. XHTML (*Extensible HTML*) is the latest and most flexible version of HTML.	Generated by WYSIWYG authoring tools such as PageBuilder, FrontPage, and Dreamweaver.
Images: .GIF, .JPG, .JPEG, .PNG	GIF or JPEG image files display as pictures on your web site. PNG files are supported by *most* but not all web browsers.	Created or formatted and saved to a web-compatible file format with image editing. Image files must be exported to GIF or JPEG format before they can be included in web pages.

Table 1-1
Most Frequently Used Elements in Web Pages

Type of File/ Filename Extension	What It Does	Where It Comes From
Audio: .AU, .RM, .WAV, .AIFF, .SWF, .MP3, .MOV, .RA, .RAM	Audio files play music or other audio content (such as interviews or speeches) in your web site.	Created with special sound editing software.
Video: .MPEG, .MOV, .AVI, .RM. .SWF	Video files present animation or movies on your web page.	Created for the web using movie editing or animation authoring.

Table 1-1
Most Frequently Used Elements in Web Pages *(continued)*

Choosing a Web Authoring Tool

Web browsers such as Internet Explorer or Netscape Navigator interpret a HTML to present formatted page content. HTML tells a browser what color to display for a page background, what size font to display, where to place an image on a page, and what page title to display in the browser title bar—just to name a few attributes that are defined by HTML.

Programs such as GeoCities PageBuilder, Microsoft FrontPage, and Macromedia Dreamweaver allow you to generate HTML using a WYSIWYG page window. FrontPage's page design window looks a lot like Microsoft Word, while Dreamweaver's interface looks more like a graphic design program. The low-budget alternative, PageBuilder, might best be described as having an interface that looks something like a low-tech video game. All three of these programs *write HTML code for you* so you don't have to learn HTML. On the other hand, if you know HTML, or you want to learn it, both FrontPage and Dreamweaver provide windows where you can see or edit HTML directly.

In addition to generating HTML, PageBuilder, FrontPage, and Dreamweaver all generate something called *Dynamic HTML*, or DHTML for short. DHTML enables pictures and text to fly around on your page or to react when a visitor interacts with your page. Rollover images that change when a visitor scrolls his or her mouse over them are an example of DHTML. You may hear the terms *CSS* (Cascading Style Sheets) and *JavaScript* in relation to web design. CSS and JavaScript are components of DHTML.

In general, web design software *does not create images for you*. Some packages come with limited clip art selections, but for most uses, you have to create your artwork using graphics software.

Creating digital images is beyond the scope of this book. However, in Chapter 3 you'll learn to prepare scanned photos and digital artwork for the web by exporting artwork to web-friendly files using web-safe colors.

Web developers sometimes refer to the HTML generated by web design programs as either *clean* or *dirty*. Clean code is HTML (and DHTML) that can more easily be interpreted and edited by someone who knows how to write code. Programs that produce relative clean code have the advantage of allowing pages to be edited by other developers, regardless of what tool was used to create the page. For instance, a page created in Dreamweaver can be easily opened in FrontPage because Dreamweaver produces relatively clean code. On the other hand, a page created in GeoCities PageBuilder will be difficult for a designer to touch-up using Dreamweaver, FrontPage, or by directly editing the HTML, because PageBuilder produces relatively dirty code.

The next section of this chapter will survey the most widely used web design software. The advantages and disadvantages of the most popular and accessible tools for creating web pages are summarized in Table 1-2.

Web Authoring Tool	Advantages	Disadvantages	Summary
GeoCities PageBuilder	Easy to use; free of charge	Limited formatting options; can be used reliably only on GeoCities sites.	Good place to start
Microsoft FrontPage	Looks like MS Word; powerful database features	Too many proprietary features	Use it if it came with your version of MS Office, or you want to get up to speed quickly in a Word-like environment
Macromedia Dreamweaver	Most powerful page design tools, ability to generate interactive and animated features with JavaScript	Difficult to learn; expensive	The choice of most web design professionals; relatively high learning curve
Adobe GoLive	Meshes well with Adobe software; sophisticated set of features	Complex interface makes frequently used features hard to find, expensive; not widely used	Equivalent in features to Dreamweaver, but not widely used; interface accessible to PhotoShop and Illustrator experts
Using a text editor to manually create HTML pages	Ultimate flexibility in page design; free	Requires learning code; does not handle file uploading	For experts only

Table 1-2
Summary of Most Widely Used Web Authoring Tools

GeoCities PageBuilder

GeoCities PageBuilder, shown in Figure 1-4, is the easiest, cheapest, and least powerful option for creating web pages. While PageBuilder does not compare to FrontPage or Dreamweaver in design capability, you can still create professional quality, attractive pages with features such as formatted text, links, embedded images, and animation.

Figure 1-4
PageBuilder's interface is intuitive and easy to use.

You don't buy or even download PageBuilder. You open PageBuilder online at the GeoCities web site, and use it to create or edit pages that were created in PageBuilder. One advantage of PageBuilder, therefore, is that you can edit your web site from any computer in the world with an Internet connection—there is no need to install software.

Many of the features available in PageBuilder work *only* with GeoCities web pages. If you want to dive into the world of web design with PageBuilder, you'll want to use either free (with display ads) or commercial sites available at *www.geocities.com*.

PageBuilder does not get along particularly well with other web design software. You *can* migrate a web site developed with PageBuilder to FrontPage or Dreamweaver, but you might end up redoing much of your page design.

PageBuilder is a fine tool for creating sites for students, classrooms, clubs, and personal sites. Use it to show off your family photos, to post the scores of your daughter's soccer league, or to share your sixth grade class's essays with parents and students. PageBuilder a great package for kids learning to design web sites. For sites that require a professional look and feel, consider using FrontPage or Dreamweaver.

FrontPage

FrontPage's menu and toolbar-based interface allows you to design web pages in an environment that will be comfortable to users of other Microsoft products like Word, PowerPoint, or Publisher (see Figure 1-5). And FrontPage integrates smoothly with other Office tools—you can easily move text, clip art, and even a PowerPoint slide show into a FrontPage web site.

Figure 1-5
FrontPage's interface is much like that of Microsoft Word and other Office applications.

FrontPage also includes the most accessible web database management tools available without programming. If running an online mailing list or managing an online discussion forum is a big part of your web plans, you will probably find FrontPage the weapon of choice. In Chapter 5, you'll learn to design pages using FrontPage.

Be forewarned, however, that if you want to take advantage of FrontPage's database features, you need to contract with a web host that supports FrontPage *extensions*—special files on the web server that are necessary for many of the most useful features of FrontPage to work. Most web hosting companies *do* provide FrontPage extensions, but if you're planning on using FrontPage, be sure to include that in your checklist when you shop for a web server. Dreamweaver MX has powerful database management tools as well (older versions of Dreamweaver require a separate program, UltraDev, to access online databases). For beginners, however, it's much easier to find web hosting companies that support the database features in FrontPage.

FrontPage retails for about $125, and recent versions run *only under the Windows operating system.* It is not available for Macs except for a very old version, FrontPage 1.0.

Dreamweaver

Dreamweaver (Figure 1-6) is the premiere choice of professional web designers because it is the most powerful software available for designing web pages. Dreamweaver generates more animation and interactivity than other web design programs, using what are called *behaviors.*

Figure 1-6
Dreamweaver is an ideal web design tool for developers who want to edit, or learn, HTML—you can display your page in both a WYSIWYG design view and code view.

Dreamweaver produces the "cleanest" HTML and therefore is preferred by professional web designers who often inspect or edit the HTML code.

The Dreamweaver community has created a wide array of additions to the program called *extensions* that are available for download at the Macromedia web site.

Dreamweaver's features come at a price—the program retails for about $400. The other price you pay to use Dreamweaver is that the software takes longer to learn than PageBuilder or even FrontPage.

If you've used graphic-design tools such as Flash or Fireworks, the interface will look familiar. But if you are more comfortable with Word, you will find the Dreamweaver environment chaotic and confusing. Even the Windows version of Dreamweaver looks more like a Macintosh program, which is fine if you're comfortable with the Mac surroundings but adds to the disorientation factor if you're more comfortable in Windows.

HTML

If you already know how to use HTML, you'll want to create your web site in Dreamweaver or FrontPage. Both these programs allow you to type HTML directly, without generating it in a WYSIWYG page editor. Dreamweaver in particular has helpful and easy-to-use HTML page editing features.

For the ultimate do-it-yourselfer, you can try to use HTML along with a separate *FTP* (File Transfer Protocol) program to move files to your remote server. If you're comfortable writing your own HTML code and using an FTP program to manage your own file transfer to a remote server, you probably don't really need this book. Instead, arm yourself with an advanced level HTML book such as Peachpit Press's *HTML for the World Wide Web with XHTML and CSS: Visual QuickStart Guide*, by Elizabeth Castro; or Osborne's *HTML: The Complete Reference*, by Thomas A. Powell.

If you use Dreamweaver or FrontPage to create your web site, you can begin to teach yourself HTML by looking at the code that gets generated as you compose and format your web pages.

The bottom line is that you can go a long way in web design and create very professional quality pages without learning HTML.

Other Software Tools You Can Use

Following are short reviews of other software tools that can be used for page design. In general, they are not widely used—which means that you won't find the kind of support and community available for PageBuilder, FrontPage, or Dreamweaver.

Adobe GoLive is similar to Dreamweaver, but with a more awkward interface and a narrow niche in the web design market. If your budget can handle the $400 required to purchase GoLive, you'll probably want to spend your money on Dreamweaver instead. The exception would be if you are an expert at other Adobe tools such as Illustrator and Photoshop, and your main criteria is a web design application that meshes most smoothly with those programs.

Macromedia Homesite is an editor for developers who are hand-coding HTML. It's for experts only.

Most Microsoft Office programs include some form of web design and web publishing features. You can use Word's Save As Web Page feature (in the File menu) to create web pages. PowerPoint and Publisher can generate web pages as well. The main drawbacks to using these programs to design web pages is that they don't provide much, if any, help in managing the process of uploading and updating files to your web server. Another problem is that the HTML (web) pages these programs generate can't easily be edited. In general, you'll have an easier time copying and pasting text and images from Word or PowerPoint to FrontPage than wrestling with the mess of files that is created when you choose the Save As Web Page features in MS Office programs.

Similarly, graphic design programs such as Fireworks, CorelDRAW, Adobe Illustrator, and Photoshop all generate web pages. The drawbacks are similar to those associated with web pages created in Microsoft Office. The pages generated by these graphic design programs are difficult to edit, and these programs don't help you transfer files to a remote web server.

If you create web pages in either Microsoft Office or by using graphic design software, your best bet is to import those files into your PageBuilder, Dreamweaver, or FrontPage web sites, and *then* transfer them to your remote server.

Chapter 2

Obtaining a
Domain Name
and Web Server

E very web site has an IP (Internet Protocol) address—something like *http://130.232.8.43/*. This address allows visitors to find your web site, and it allows you to upload content to your site. When you contract with a Internet site provider for web hosting, your provider will create a web site for you and assign it an IP address.

The problem is, nobody is going to remember a web address in IP address format. Instead, sites are known by their domain names, which are associated with an IP address. Domain names follow the *www.* in the URL (Uniform Resource Locator) that you use to call up a web site. For example, the domain name for a site where you can purchase your own domain name is *www.register.com*. Unless your web site is intended only for a small audience (for instance, an intranet used for transferring or sharing files within your organization), you'll want to associate an easy-to-remember domain name with your IP address.

Most web site providers combine the process of renting web server space and purchasing a domain name. They do this by working with companies that register domain names. When you contract for web server space, your host will give you instructions on how to associate your domain name with the IP address provided by the web host.

Because associating a domain name with an IP address can be a bit of a hassle for a beginning-level web designer, the simplest way to get a domain name is to do it through your web host provider. When you begin the process of ordering web space, most providers will ask whether you need a domain name, and then they'll guide you through the process of signing up for one.

Registering a Domain Name

You can grab a domain name even before you shop for a web host, or you can sign up for a web name *while* you contract for web server space. In the latter case, you'll usually be routed through the process of choosing a domain name even before you select other features for your web site. In other words, one way or another, you'll probably start out by buying a domain name.

Don't count on getting your first choice of domain names. If you were hoping that a name like *autoinsurance.com*, *poetry.com*, or *wine.com* was available, for example, you're too late. Those names, and millions more, have already been taken.

Domain name vendors will offer you two options if your first choice of domain names is taken. You can try your domain name with an *extension* other than the popular "dot-com" (.com). Other popular domain name extensions for sites associated with the United States are .net and .org. Yet other extensions, such as .tv, .info, or .us (the latter usually associated with sites only in the United States), are often available. So, even though wine.com was registered long ago, wine.info, wine.org, or wine.tv might still be available.

Your other option is to explore whether domain names similar to your first choice are available with the extension you prefer. A wine dealer might want to determine whether winebargains.com is available, for example. If your first choice for a domain name is taken, domain name registration companies will help you choose from options that are close to your preferred name, as shown in Figure 2-1.

Figure 2-1
Registering a domain name

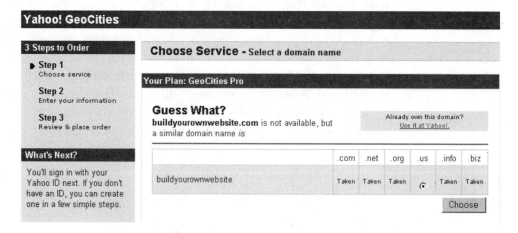

If you register your own domain name, avoid fly-by-night registration companies. While it's not always the cheapest, you're probably best off going to *www.register.com* to sign up for a domain name on your own. Unreliable domain registration companies have been known to sell a domain name to a competing company when it expires, without notifying the original domain name owner.

Domain name registration generally costs about $15 per year, but you can often get a discount if you sign up for a multiple-year deal. Domain name registration companies always require a credit card number, a contact person for the site, and a technical contact person for the site. So have this information handy when you start to shop.

Ownership of a domain name can be a touchy issue. Domain names are usually associated with an individual, so companies or organizations should make a conscious decision about whose name will be used to register a site.

Shopping for a Web Host

Thousands of companies are ready to host your web site on their servers. They range from companies that provide free, small sites with limited features and pop-up ads, to complex sites loaded with features for providing fast-downloading video and (relatively) hacker-proof security.

Web-hosting options are cloaked in technical terminology such as *bandwidth*, *scripting*, *SSL*, and *subdomains*. Unfortunately, you'll need a basic understanding of these and other features to buy just the right amount, and the right kind, of web server space. These terms, and others, will be explained in this chapter.

How much should you expect to pay for web hosting? The cheapest reliable sites without pop-up or banner ads start at around $5 per month and are sufficient for web sites with a dozen or so pages' full of images. Three factors will add to the cost of your site:

❏ If you need to store more files and larger files, you'll need *more server space.*

❏ If too many people are visiting your site or you need to upload more files more often to your site, you'll need *more bandwidth.*

❏ If you plan to collect data in an online database, or you want to provide streaming (fast-downloading) video, for example, you'll need to pay extra for *more features* at your site.

The following sections of this chapter will help you prepare a shopping list so you can purchase the perfect web host.

What about the free site that came with your Internet service provider (ISP)—like AOL or Earthlink? These sites have the advantage of being free, and these ISPs don't clutter the site with ads. They usually come with their own software to generate pages. But the web site that came with your ISP is probably too small and primitive for even a sophisticated personal site. It won't work well with FrontPage, Dreamweaver, or GeoCities' PageBuilder. If you want a site with a custom domain name, with dozens of large images, with input forms, or with large files like audio and video, you'll need more web hosting than what can be provided by your ISP.

For example, AOL's "My Place" personal web sites allow you only 2MB for your site. By comparison, the web page shown in Figure 2-2, and the linked full-sized photos associated with it, is about 4MB in size.

Figure 2-2
A 4MB web page

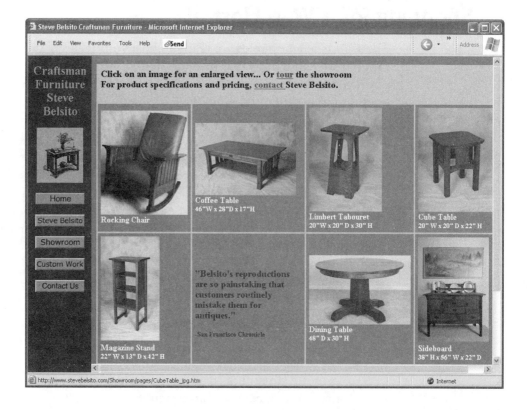

How Much Bandwidth Do You Need?

Bandwidth is a measure of how much information will be sent to and from your web site. Each time a visitor visits your site, he or she will download files to see your pages and pictures, listen to your audio files, or watch your videos. The more visitors at your site, the more bandwidth you need, since more visitors mean more files being downloaded from the server. In addition, the larger your site files, the more bandwidth you'll need.

You also use up your allotted bandwidth by uploading files to your server. Normally, the process of creating and updating your site doesn't use up a whole lot of bandwidth, but if you're uploading a new 5-minute QuickTime video every day, for example, you'll need to factor that into how much bandwidth you'll need.

The quantity of information sent back and forth from your site is measured in gigabytes (GB, for short). If you're expecting hundreds, not thousands, of visitors a day, 10GB per month should be fine. If you are planning a commercial site and expecting thousands of people to download images every day, you might start with 35GB per month.

The fact is, it's pretty difficult to guess accurately how much bandwidth you'll need. If you expect your site to grow, look for a provider that will let you easily increase bandwidth as your site and traffic grow. Start with the smallest bandwidth available, and then upgrade when your provider notifies you that you're getting near the allowable file transfer limit.

Buying Server Space

Server space is a little easier to calculate than bandwidth. You can get out your calculator and total up the size of the image and media files you want to upload to your site, and then shop for that much server space.

Server space is measured in megabytes (MB). A small site might squeeze into 5MB of server space, while a moderately sized commercial site will probably need 500MB.

As with contracting for bandwidth, choose a provider that lets you easily increase your space without paying a penalty for adding space on the fly. Figure 2-3 shows three different web site packages with varying amounts of included web server space and bandwidth.

Figure 2-3
Yahoo! provides
sites with varying
bandwidth and
server space.

	Starter	Standard	Professional
	Sign Up	Sign Up	Sign Up
Price			
Monthly service fee	$11.95	$19.95	$39.95
One-time setup fee	$15.00	$25.00	$25.00
Personalized Domain Name			
Free registration for your own domain name	Yes	Yes	Yes
Matching email accounts	10	25	35
Business Edition email		Yes	Yes
Matching web site subdomains	10	15	15
Customer Support			
24/7 toll-free phone support		Yes	Yes
Online Help site	Yes	Yes	Yes
Priority email	Yes	Yes	Yes
For Your Visitors			
Data transfer (bandwidth)	20 GB	25 GB	35 GB
Customizable site search	Yes	Yes	Yes
Customizable error pages	Yes	Yes	Yes
Web Site Management			
Disk space for storing files	50 MB	100 MB	350 MB

Bandwidth → Data transfer (bandwidth)

Server space → Disk space for storing files

Getting Help

One of the most underrated features of a web host is support. When things aren't working right, you'll appreciate the level of support provided by your host.

Live technical support is one of the most expensive features you can add to a web site, and it usually comes only on sites that cost more than $50 per month. Other features can simply be programmed into the site software, but live support requires paying people who have technical expertise and communications skills. Unfortunately, live phone tech support from your web-hosting company is probably out of the price range of many beginning-level web designers.

Even e-mail tech support is not included in many web host packages. If it is, it's a good value. Try testing the tech support e-mail link at a prospective provider *before* you contract for service. Send an e-mail saying you're interested in the provider's hosting service, and ask a technical question about the company's hosting (use the information in this chapter to pose a good question). Then see how long you wait for a response and how helpful the response is.

To their credit, many large hosting companies do have extensive online support in the form of articles, search features, and sometimes online user forums. If you have to settle for this level of support, explore your provider's site and see how useful the information is.

Security Issues

For most beginner-level web designers, web security is not a big issue because *hackers* (people who break into web sites without authorization to steal information) are probably not going to be focused on infiltrating your site and stealing information from your server. However, security is an extra precaution that may pay off when you really need it.

Password Protection

If you plan to include content that is restricted to registered users, for example, you can add password protection to your site. This feature usually costs extra. Web-design software, such as FrontPage or Dreamweaver, cannot provide password protection unless that feature is part of your web host package.

If your provider includes password protection as part of your service, you'll still need instructions on how to make selected files or pages in your site password protected. Some hosting companies require that you provide a list of usernames and passwords for protected pages. Others allow you to define users and passwords on your own. If this feature is important to you, ask your host to explain how its service works *before* you sign up for server space.

Secure Socket Layer

Secure Socket Layer (SSL) provides extra security for confidential web transactions. It's probably not something you need for your personal site. If you attach e-commerce features to your site, however, you'll contract with a company that sets up a shopping cart interface with a server that protects buyers from having their credit card information stolen. Companies such as Yahoo!, bCentral, and PDG provide e-commerce, and their servers have the SSL protocol, which provides encrypted data transfer to protect sensitive information such as credit card numbers.

E-commerce providers allow you to customize the pages used for your orders so that visitors will not need to be aware that they are actually leaving *your* server and moving to the e-commerce server when they make a purchase. Visitors will be alerted by their browsers that they are going to (or from) a secure server, but it won't be obvious or important to them that this SSL server is not the same one you use for your main web hosting.

Server Features for Intense Media

If you plan to include audio or video at your site, you'll need a *lot* of server space. Media files require hundreds of times more server space than image files. File sizes for typical media files are measured in kilobytes (KB). The graph shown in Figure 2-4 compares the file sizes of various media files with that of regular image files.

Figure 2-4
Comparing media files with regular image files. These are typical file sizes in kilobytes.

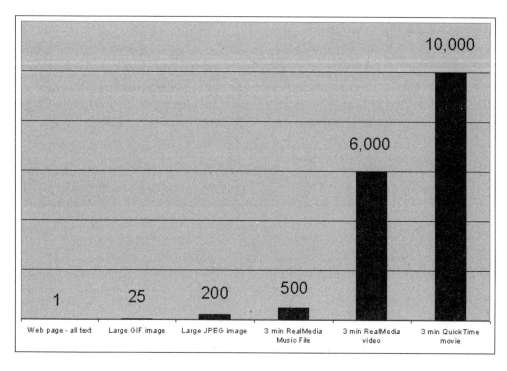

If you're really serious about letting visitors download video from your site, you will want to contract for web server space that supports either the RealMedia server or the QuickTime Streaming Server. This server software allows downloading media to *buffer* (download before playing) efficiently so that viewers can see the best quality video with the shortest possible wait.

TIPS OF THE TRADE

You Might Not Need a Special Server for Your Video

It is possible to deliver streaming media, such as video or audio, without using streaming servers. If you are putting up a handful of streaming media files for download, streaming servers should not be necessary. If you are broadcasting live streams, or you need to support large numbers of simultaneous access, however, these servers are critical.

Using Subdomains

Subdomains allow each department (or individual) in an organization to have its own domain name. For example, the University of East Dakota could have domain names for each department, such as www.history.uofeastdakota.edu, www.math.uofeastdakota.edu, or www.sports.uofeastdakota.edu.

Web hosting that allows you to set up subdomains usually costs extra. Some providers allow you to configure your site to set up subdomains yourself by going to their web site and using special web consoles available for hosting clients. Others require that you provide them with the name of the subdomain, and they handle the process of defining new subdomains. Figure 2-5 shows the price list from one web site provider, with most packages including subwebs as an option.

Figure 2-5
AtFreeWeb.com
offers sites with
or without
subdomains.

Most packages
include
subwebs ———

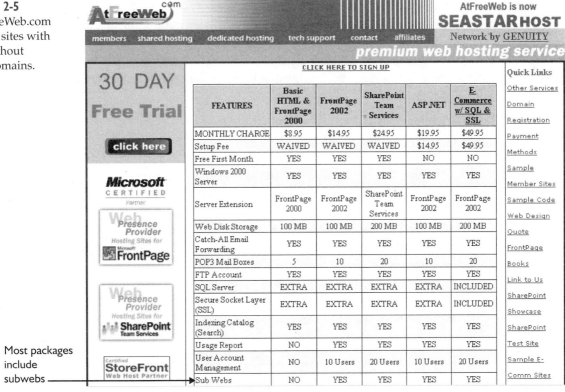

Collecting Data with Server Scripts

Server *scripting* is used to create web sites that react dynamically with information in an online database. For instance, a visitor might sign up on your mailing list and then get a confirmation e-mail while his or her contact information is added to a database at your server. That database can then generate reports for your use, or it can be used to send out e-mail to everyone on your list.

Other, even more complex, server scripting applications use databases to provide site content. For example, a web site might display a list of available products that changes each time a product is purchased. This is an advanced type of web site and requires a team of expert programmers and database managers to set up and administer.

To be clear, *you* don't create server scripts. Writing server scripts is a specialized skill. However, many boilerplate server scripts are available. You can find these scripts on the Internet, and most web-hosting companies have some available for your use. Chapter 7 explains in detail how to integrate several useful CGI scripts into your web pages.

You can use a number of methods for collecting information at your site to use in mailing lists or online forums (such as threaded discussions). These methods are premade and require no knowledge of the underlying scripting. Such options include FrontPage extensions, premade Common Gateway Interface (CGI) scripts, and scripts from companies that provide data-processing tools that interact with your site but are designed and maintained at another server. The following section will introduce some of these options, and they will be explained in detail in later chapters.

Managing Data with FrontPage Extensions

One of the easiest ways for beginning web designers to collect and manage data is to use FrontPage and purchase server space from a web host that provides FrontPage *extensions*. Extensions are special applications that provide additional functionality to a program. Because FrontPage is the most widely used tool for web design, thousands of web hosts support FrontPage extensions.

FrontPage extensions allow you to collect information in forms, and then you can perform three tasks with the data you collect:

❑ You can have information sent to you in e-mail.

❑ You can have the data displayed on a web page (for instance, in a guest book).

❑ You can save the data to an Access database or an Excel worksheet.

FrontPage 98, 2000, and 2002 each has its own set of extensions, so if you are using FrontPage 2002, for example, look for a provider that includes FrontPage 2002 extensions.

Using CGI to Manage Form Data

CGI scripts are programs written in languages such as Perl that are used by your web server to manage the data that visitors submit in forms at your site.

Most web-hosting companies—those that provide more than rock-bottom service—include a set of CGI scripts for you to use. These scripts typically collect data submitted by a visitor and send that data to you as an e-mail.

CGI scripts provided by web hosts are often paired with forms. You copy some HTML (Hypertext Markup Language, the language used to communicate on the Internet) code provided by a hosting company into your web page, and that one-step process creates a form and inserts on your page the code that's necessary to capture data and send it to you.

Custom Server Scripting

Beyond premade CGI scripts and FrontPage extensions, web-hosting companies offer support for those who want to create their own server scripting using Active ServerPages (ASP), Java ServerPages (JSP), and other server languages.

If you are designing a web site for a large company or organization that has a team of expert web-database designers, as well as a crew of experts at server scripting, you'll want to consult with them on what server scripting options they can use. At the other end of the spectrum, many small businesses, nonprofits, schools, and other institutions can utilize free CGI script packages that are covered in Chapter 7.

Shared vs. Dedicated Servers

A web *sever*—a combination of a large computer and special server software—usually manages many web sites. Each of these web sites "shares" one server but has its own domain name and its own URL and IP address, and it can be custom configured with features like SSL for confidential transactions, subdomains, or CGI scripts. For most organizations, nonprofits, schools, individuals, and small businesses, a shared server (also referred to as a *virtual* server site) is the rational choice.

Only a large company with its own expert server administrators need or can manage a *dedicated* server that supports only its single web site.

E-mail Included

Almost all web-hosting packages include e-mail addresses. Typically, small sites will offer five addresses, and larger sites will offer more. For instance, if your domain name is www.cheapredwine.us, you might want to set up accounts for your sales department (sales@cheapredwine.us), technical support (techsupport@cheapredwine.us), quality issues (qualityissues@cheapredwine.us), and so on.

Many web-hosting companies provide a page that you can log into and set up your own e-mail addresses. Others require you to e-mail the tech support staff to create new e-mail addresses.

Making Your Server Shopping List

Now that you've been introduced to the main features available from web-hosting providers, it's time to sit down with your scratch pad and make a list of the features *you* will need as you shop for hosting. In general, you're best off looking for web hosts that provide easy options for upgrading your site so that later on you can add features like subdomains or password-protected pages, even if you don't need them now.

You can get a good, starter web site for your small business or organization for less than $10 a month. Avoid the absolute bottom-end host providers—the ones that promise "$1 web hosting" or other deals that are literally too good to be true. Companies that claim to provide you with sites that cheap will stick you with hidden costs, and the sites they provide will be unreliable.

If your budget doesn't allow you to pay even $5 a month for web hosting, start with a free site from *www.geocities.com* or one of the other free hosts you'll find searching the web for free web sites. These free providers include pop-up or banner ads on your pages, but they do provide web hosting for folks with the most bare-bones budgets.

Companies that provide free hosting include freeservers (*www.freeservers.com*) and Yahoo! GeoCities (*www.geocities.com*). Other options are listed at *http://www.freewebspace.net/*.

You can find a list of links to reliable web-hosting companies, as well as sites that list and rate web hosts at the companion site for this book, www.buildyourownwebsite.us.

Use Table 2-1 to create your own list of features, and then start searching the web for good hosting deals.

Element	What It Is	How Much Do You Need?	Summary
Bandwidth	How much information can be sent back and forth to your site (measured in gigabytes—GB).	10GB/month for a starter site with some media files; 35GB/month for a commercial site with e-commerce.	Look for a provider that will let you increase bandwidth as your site and traffic grow.
Server space	How much content you can store at your site (measured in megabytes).	Small site—5MB; moderately sized commercial site—500 MB.	Choose a provider that lets you increase space on the fly without paying a penalty.

Table 2-1
Web Host Shopping Guide

Element	What It Is	How Much Do You Need?	Summary
E-mail addresses	Custom e-mail addresses at your domain name.	Most sites provide at least five e-mail addresses.	If you need lots of e-mail addresses, make sure you can add them as an optional part of your hosting package.
FrontPage extensions	Files that manage form data in online databases and other features in FrontPage.	FrontPage 98, 2000, and 2002 have their own sets of extensions; look for the latest version.	Good if you will be including an Access database in your FrontPage site.
CGI scripts	Used to manage form data for products other than FrontPage.	Different web hosts provide their own sets of forms and scripts.	Even if you aren't including data, this feature may come in handy as your site grows in complexity.
Support	Help provided by your web host—don't assume *any* unless specified.	Ranges from auto-replay e-mail support to 24/7 live phone assistance.	Decide how much hand-holding you need, and try to test the support before purchasing server space.
Password protection	Pages that can be accessed only by visitors with a username and password.	Used for sharing confidential or internal information.	An available option for larger sites that will have restricted areas for registered users only.
Real Media Server and/or QuickTime Server	Software that detects connection speeds and makes different versions of your movies available to dial-up and DSL visitors.	Site providers with RealMedia's Server provide support for multiple streams (download speeds). Hosting services with QuickTime Streaming Server support buffered media downloading for QuickTime and Windows media files.	Useful if your site will be heavy on audio or video.
Subdomains	Additional level of domain name.	Example: www.store.z.com would be a subdomain of www.z.com.	Useful for organizations (like universities) with many departments or divisions.

Table 2-1
Web Host Shopping Guide *(continued)*

Element	What It Is	How Much Do You Need?	Summary
SSL	Provides extra security for confidential web transactions.	Often offered as part of larger web site packages. Most sites don't need this.	Commercial e-commerce vendors like Yahoo!, bCentral, or PDG provide secure servers; beginners don't need SSL on their own sites.
PHP/MySQL, ASP, JSP, and other server languages	Used for developing complex database-driven web sites.	Not for beginners or intermediate developers.	Check with your organization's database administrator to see if he or she will help you implement a database-driven web and which server language he or she prefers.

Table 2-1
Web Host Shopping Guide *(continued)*

Where to Shop

Once you know which features you want in a web site, you can search the Internet for providers that will support the features you need. For example, if you're into web video, and you plan to include a bunch of RealMedia video files, try searching for "web hosting RealMedia G2 server." Or, if you need hosting with a nice supply of CGI scripts, search for "web hosting CGI scripts." Keep in mind that you can always consult the updated listing of web hosts at the book's web site—*www.buildyourownwebsite.us*.

Chapter 3

Gathering Web Content

Tools of the Trade

You can create web content using a wide variety of software. Any text editor, including Microsoft Word, will do a fine job of creating and editing text destined for your web site. If you plan to include photos, you'll need to scan them onto your computer's hard drive with a scanner or have them processed digitally so you can import them from a CD. For the most part, you'll be able to collect and format web content using free software that comes with your computer and—if you have them—your scanner and digital camera.

In Chapter 1, you learned to organize your web site's content by designing a basic flow chart. That chart should include the information and images you want to include on your *home* page (the opening page on your site) as well as a plan for what content will be available on other pages in your site. The flow chart forces you to make decisions about what is the most important information at your site and what other information is going to be available.

Your web site plan should provide a way for visitors to navigate between pages in your site using *links*. These links are usually depicted in site flow charts using arrows between pages in your site.

Of course, as you actually design your web pages, you will think of ways to improve on your original plan and make changes. But your site will be much more accessible and usable if you work from a basic overview of your entire site.

Once you have created a plan for your web site, one more important preparatory stage must occur before you dive into laying out your web pages: you must collect all the *files* you need for your site. In this chapter, you'll learn to prepare text, image, audio, and video files for your web site by adapting the content for the

31

web and saving these files to appropriate file formats. In the following chapters, you'll learn to plug text, audio, and video into your web pages.

Preparing Text for Web Pages

Generally speaking, text content that is prepared for web pages is shorter than similar content that is intended for printed output. Web pages do a great job of integrating text, color pictures, and other media (such as audio and video), but it's difficult to read large amounts of text on the web, for several reasons.

Web text is *grainier* than printed text because the resolution of computer monitors is much lower than that of even a low-cost desktop printer. Inkjet or laser printers usually print text at between 300 and 600 *dpi* (dots per inch), while computer monitors generally display between 72 and 96 dpi. Small fonts are particularly difficult to read on a computer monitor.

In addition, it's just more convenient to read large amounts of text in a book than it is to read a book on the web. This is one reason why e-books are a long way from displacing printed books. If you need to present large amounts of text at your web site, consider exporting the text to PDF (Portable Document File)—as explained later in this chapter in the section "Preparing PDF Files for the Web."

You can easily copy text from any file into a web page. Depending on the program you use to format your web pages, some or none of the formatting will be preserved. As a general rule, you'll want your text pretty much unformatted before you copy and paste it into your web pages.

If your text is saved as a Microsoft Word file, or any other file format (such as TXT or RTF), it will be easy to import into your web page using the tools explored in the next three chapters.

When you place text on a web page, you'll be able to assign fonts to that text in your web page editing software. However, keep in mind that a visitor to your web site will be able to see the fonts you assign to your text *only* if he or she has *those fonts* installed on his or her operating system. For that reason, web fonts are pretty much restricted to some variety of Courier, Arial/Helvetica, and Times. More fancy fonts will be converted to one of these more basic font styles when viewed by visitors who have different fonts than you do.

If you need to display a special font in your web site—for instance, in your organization's name or logo—you can do this by converting the text to a graphic.

Limit Your Use of Graphical Text

Using graphical text can have many drawbacks. It downloads more slowly than "real" text. It cannot be copied or pasted, and it is more difficult to print than regular text. And content displayed as graphical text is not recognized by search engines. For these reasons, it's best to avoid large blocks of graphical text and use it only to format text with a unique font. More instructions on how to create graphical text are found later in this chapter in the section "Creating Graphical Text."

Preparing Photos for the Web

One of the challenges of presenting photos on a web site is that, as mentioned earlier in this chapter, computer monitors display images at much lower resolutions than printed photos. Photos that must be displayed with fine detail will not look good on the web, where viewers will see them at up to 100 times less dpi resolution than a high-quality printed photo. Keep this in mind as you select photos for your web site.

Digital photos for the web can come from a digital camera, or you can convert regular photos to digital files by scanning them. In either case, you'll need to save them as a web-friendly file format before you can use them in your web site.

Edit Your Photos Before You Add Them to Your Web Page

Generally speaking, you'll want to edit your photos *before* you start working on your web page. The web design software options explored in the following chapters provide *some* features for resizing and, in some cases, tinting or cropping images. But those features are limited, and even when you use them, you'll find that the more your image is edited in advance, the more smoothly it will embed in your web page.

Images can be edited using special graphics software. Image editing can include cropping (cutting off edges of the image), resizing, and editing the color intensity, contrast, and even tint. Image editing software ranges from the powerful but complex Adobe Photoshop (which retails for more than $600), to the image editing software that comes free with scanners, digital cameras, or operating systems.

For many web sites, the free graphics software that came with your scanner or digital camera is fine for editing, sizing, and saving images for the web. Don't be too quick to drop hundreds of extra dollars on Photoshop until you're sure you've stretched the limits of simpler and cheaper software.

In the following sections of this chapter, you'll learn to scan, crop, resize, and save images using the free Paint program that comes with Microsoft Windows XP. The versions of Paint that are included with older versions of Windows and Macintosh computers are similar. In the "Saving Images for the Web" section of this chapter, you'll learn to use file compression and downloading options to further reduce your file size and improve picture download time.

Scanning Photos

If your images were shot with a digital camera or were processed onto a CD, you can open them directly with a graphics software program. If you are including printed photos on your site, you can scan them.

When you plug a scanner into your computer, the current generation of operating systems automatically allow you to access your scanner through any graphics software you have installed on your computer. So, for example, if you use Windows 98, Windows Me, Windows 2000, or Windows XP, you can scan images using the free Paint software program or any other graphics program (such as Photoshop).

Here's how to scan a photo in Windows Paint or import a file from your digital camera: First, choose File | From Scanner or Camera.

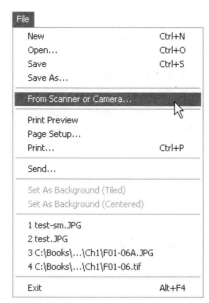

You'll see a list of all your installed scanners and digital cameras (if more than one), and you can select which device to use. The next steps will depend on the software that comes with your scanner or digital camera, but generally you will be able to preview and then import (from a camera) or scan your photo.

The process is similar in other graphics programs. For instance, in Photoshop you choose File | Import, and then choose an installed scanner or digital camera from a list, as shown in Figure 3-1.

Figure 3-1
Scanning a photo in Photoshop

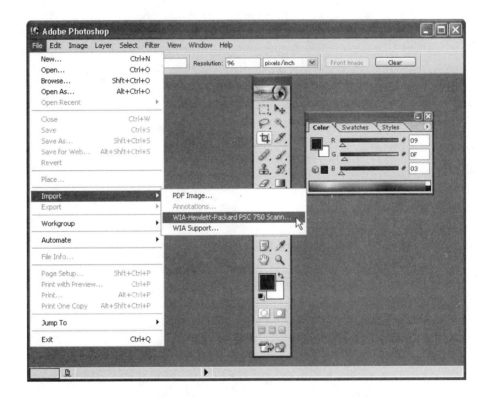

Once you've scanned an image or imported an image from your digital camera, you need to edit that image so that it will display well on the web. Then save it to a web-compatible file format (such as JPEG or GIF).

TIPS OF THE TRADE

How Important Is Resolution?

When you shop for a scanner or digital camera, you'll find many options for resolution density. *Resolution* means how many *pixels*—dots containing image information—per inch are generated. These statistics are not relevant for digital images destined for the web, where the highest resolution is only about 100 pixels per inch (ppi).

Cropping and Sizing Photos

When you choose a size for your photo, keep in mind that larger images take longer to download. That means a beautiful 8×6 color photo that looks great on your computer might tie up a visitor's computer for minutes while he or she waits for the picture to load. Long waits like that will drive visitors away from your site.

Cropping (trimming off sections of the top, bottom, or sides of a picture) and resizing (to make a picture smaller) are two methods you can use to reduce the file size of your images. Smaller file size means faster downloads.

One technique for displaying large images is to place a small *thumbnail* version of the image on your web page, and make that small image a clickable link to a larger version of your photo, as shown in Figure 3-2.

Figure 3-2
Using a thumbnail image as a link to a full-sized image

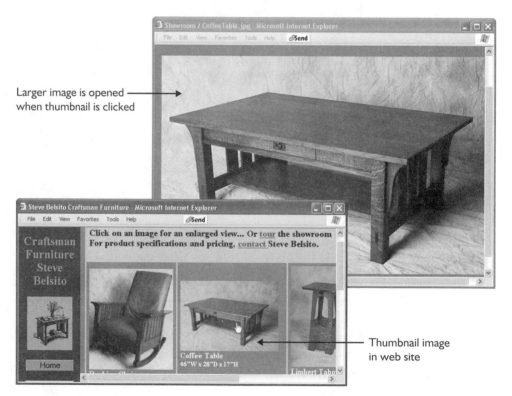

Larger image is opened when thumbnail is clicked

Thumbnail image in web site

Cropping Photos

Almost any image editing program, including the free ones that come with your operating system, allow you to resize or crop an image. Both cropping and resizing an image to make it smaller reduce the amount of information stored in the file that conveys that image over the web.

To crop a photo in Paint, choose the Select tool in the toolbox and click and drag to draw a marquee around the portion of the image you want to *include* in the cropped photo, as shown in Figure 3-3. Choose Edit | Copy to save that section of the photo to the clipboard. Choose File | New to create a new document, and then choose Edit | Paste to paste in the cropped image.

Figure 3-3
Selecting an area
to crop in Paint

To crop an image in Photoshop, click the Crop tool in the toolbox, and draw a marquee around the section of the image you want to keep, as shown in Figure 3-4. Click the Crop tool again and confirm your crop in the dialog box.

Figure 3-4
Cropping a photo
in Photoshop

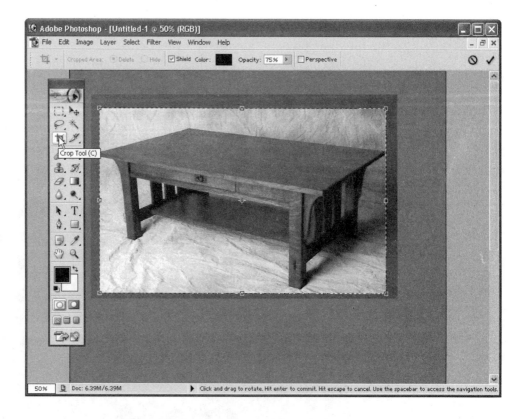

Sophisticated image editing software allows you the option of *resizing* an image or *resampling* the image. Resizing, in programs such as Photoshop, makes the image smaller but retains all the information needed to resize the image to its original dimensions. Resampling an image *does not* retain this information. To reduce file size, choose the Resampling checkbox when you resize in Photoshop.

Resizing Photos

When you resize a photo for the web, you almost always make it *smaller*. That's because printed images, particularly an 8×10 or larger image, are too big to fit on web pages and too slow for visitors to download. Beyond that, enlarging an image generally makes that image grainy and blurry, and the quality is not satisfactory.

If You Need to Enlarge a Photo…

Sophisticated photo editing programs like Photoshop do allow you to make photos larger using a variety of techniques to generate new pixels.

To resize an open photo in Paint, choose Image | Stretch/Skew to open the dialog box shown next. To maintain the same height-to-width ratio in your reduced size image, enter the same percent value in both the Horizontal and Vertical Stretch boxes, and then click OK. So, for example, if you wanted to create an image a quarter the size of the original, you'd enter **25** (for 25 percent) in both the Horizontal and Vertical Stretch boxes.

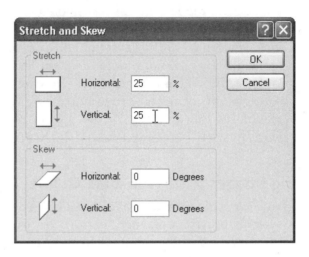

Professional-quality photo editing programs like Photoshop provide an option for resampling when you resize an image. If you want to reduce your file size, *do* select the resampling option or checkbox in your software when you resize. Turning off resampling maintains all the information required to produce the full-sized image, but it does not reduce file size.

Keep a Backup Copy of Your Original Image File!

In general, the file size reduction techniques discussed here cannot be reversed. When you crop a photo or resize it to make it smaller, you cannot later reattach the cropped elements or enlarge an image to its original size. Generally speaking, when image editing software saves a cropped or resized image, only the information needed for the cropped and resized image is saved. The most basic way to protect yourself in case you ever need the full-sized image is to save the original digital photo or keep a safe copy of the original printed photo. That way, you can always start back from your full-size, uncropped photo if you need to.

Creating Digital Artwork for the Web

If you are artistically endowed enough to design your own logos and other graphics for your web site, you'll want to keep in mind a few basic rules that will make your artwork look good on a web page. Web photos, web logos, icons, and other artwork should be as small in size as possible to allow them to download quickly.

Remember that all web artwork displays at a low resolution on monitors. Avoid designing images that use very fine detail. Although that detail might reproduce well on a 600 dpi laser printer or inkjet printer, it will be *lost* when the image is reproduced at 75–100 dpi on a web page.

The final thing to keep in mind when you design graphics for your web page is that various operating systems and monitors display colors differently. What looks like gray on your monitor might look closer to blue on someone else's laptop. And with all the new web-viewing devices entering the market, some colors might not display properly at all. Artwork for the web should be confined to what are called *web-safe colors*—a set of 216 colors that display reliably on the widest variety of operating and display systems.

Designing Images with Web-Safe Colors

Web-safe colors are displayed most reliably on the widest variety of operating systems, browsers, and hardware. If, for example, you use a non–web-safe color in your artwork, that color will likely be converted to *a different* color when it appears on a Palm Pilot, Web TV, or some other nonconventional Internet display device.

You can find a display and listing of all web-safe colors, along with their RGB (red-green-blue) values at *www.lynda.com/hexh.html*, shown next. This page is part of a web site maintained by web color guru Lynda Weinman, and the site includes other valuable advice on using colors in web sites. If you have a color printer, it will be helpful to print this page for reference. If not, bookmark it in your browser if you plan to design images for the web.

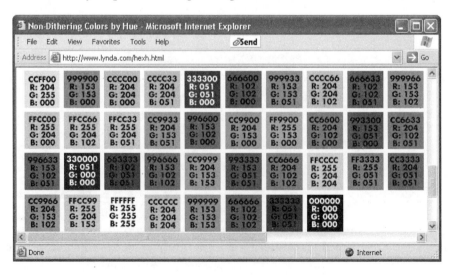

Professional image editing software like Adobe Illustrator, CorelDRAW, or Adobe Photoshop comes with settings that allow you to restrict your color palette to web-safe colors. Other programs require you to make sure your images use web-safe colors.

To constrain your color set to web-safe colors in Adobe Illustrator, choose Web Color Sliders from the Color Palette menu, as shown in Figure 3-5. To choose the web-safe color palette in Adobe Photoshop, choose Web Safe RGB from the Color Palette menu. For other image editing programs, consult the help program to find out how to enable the web-safe color palette before you create web graphics.

Figure 3-5
Choosing the web-safe color palette in Adobe Photoshop 7

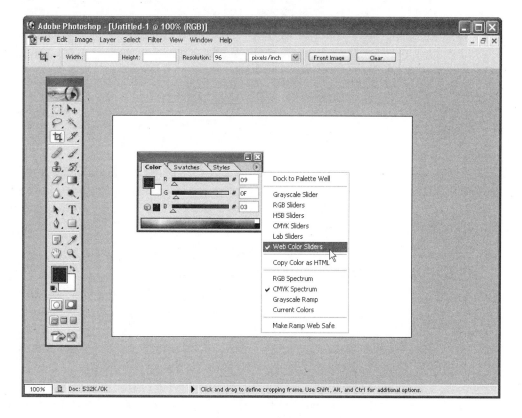

If you're working with a low-budget graphic design program (and that's fine), you can manually define web-safe colors. For example, in Microsoft Paint, choose Colors | Edit Colors. In the Edit Colors palette, click Define Custom Colors. Use the values for red, green, and blue that you looked up at *www.lynda.com*, as shown in Figure 3-6.

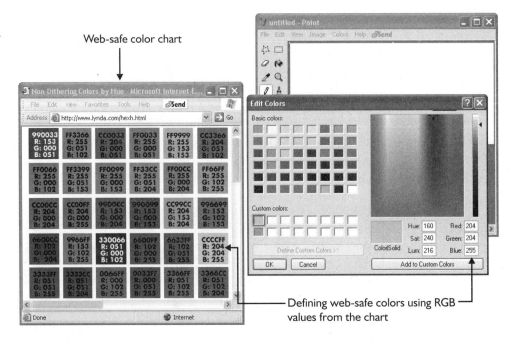

Figure 3-6
Defining your own web-safe colors in Paint using RGB values from www.lynda.com

Web-safe color chart

Defining web-safe colors using RGB values from the chart

Now that you've configured your image editing software for web-safe colors, you can design navigation buttons and logos for your site. Just remember to keep images as small as possible, avoid images that require fine detail when displayed, and stick to web-safe colors.

Creating Graphical Text

If you need to include fonts outside the short list of those supported by most operating systems (Courier, Times, and Arial/Helvetica), you'll want to create that text in your graphics program and save it as an image. In this way, you ensure that the text will display at the exact size and font that you assign, regardless of the visitor's operating system or installed font set.

To create graphical text, use the Text tool in your graphics program to type text, as shown in Figure 3-7. Then save that image. The text you create can't be edited later, and it can't be copied and pasted as text from your web page. But it *will* preserve all your sizing and formatting.

Figure 3-7
Creating graphical
text in Paint—the
text fonts will be
preserved in any
browser and any
operating system.

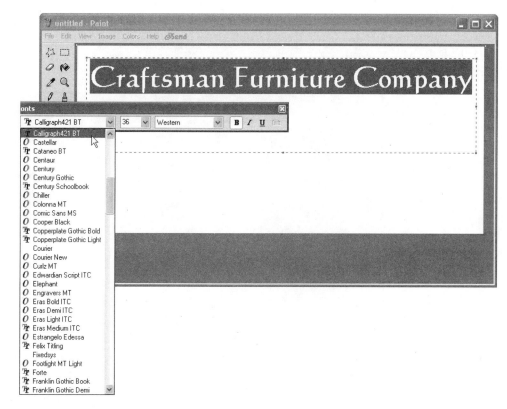

Saving Images for the Web

If you create images for the web, you'll need to save them in your image editing
program in web-friendly file formats. If you already have graphic images, such
as a company logo or an icon that is used by your organization, you can convert
these images to formats that work on the web.

The two universally supported web graphic file formats are GIF and JPEG.
Digital art software uses many other file formats (like TIFF and BMP, for example),
but those formats are used for hardcopy printed output and not for web graphics.

Sophisticated image editing software like Photoshop or Illustrator will offer
you many options for saving your images as GIF or JPEG files. (Note that the
PNG format is also widely supported by web browsers, but not quite as universally as the GIF and JPEG formats.) Other, more basic image editing software,
might simply provide the option of saving your images as either GIF or JPEG.
Figure 3-8 shows an image being saved as a GIF file.

Figure 3-8
Saving a page banner
as a GIF file in Paint

In general, JPEG is the best format for saving photographs and GIF is best for saving artwork such as logos, icons, and banners for your web site. The JPEG format does a better job of handling the large number of colors found in photos, and the GIF format is well suited to artwork with a relatively small number of colors.

Professional image editors allow you to select just part of the screen to save. However, if you are saving an image in Paint, you must resize the white background area so it is not larger than the image itself. Do this by dragging on the corner of the white area to resize it to fit your image.

If you are creating artwork or editing photos in sophisticated software like Photoshop, you will have many options beyond just choosing GIF or JPEG. If you save to GIF format, you can make one color *transparent*—so that your web page background color will show through the image. GIF images can also be *interlaced* so that they fade in, in phases, instead of appearing on a web page as stripes, from top to bottom, while a visitor waits for the image to download. JPEG image files can have a similar feature, but with JPEGs it's called *progressive imaging*.

JPEG image files can be compressed to make them download faster. But while more compression means smaller file sizes, it also means lower quality.

Professional-quality graphics software applications, such as Illustrator and Photoshop, allow you to define web graphics options (shown in Table 3-1) after you choose a file format. Choose File | Save For Web in Illustrator or Photoshop to see a preview of your image as you adjust features such as compression, as shown in Figure 3-9.

File Format	Feature	What It Does
GIF	Transparency	Allows you to define a color that will be "knocked out" of the image and will be replaced by the background color of your web page.
GIF	Interlacing	Allows images to "fade in" while a visitor waits for them to download. Useful for large images or for visitors with slow Internet connections.
JPEG	Progressive	Similar to interlacing with GIFs.
JPEG	Compression	More compression reduces file size but also reduces quality. Medium, or 50% compression, is appropriate for most web photos.

Table 3-1
Web Graphic Options

Figure 3-9
Saving a photo as a JPEG file with progressive fade-in and 50% compression in Photoshop's Save For Web window

Assign Links to Images

Sophisticated image editing programs sometimes include options that allow you to assign such web attributes as links to images. Usually there's no need to worry about these features in your image editor. You can assign web graphic attributes like links more easily when you create your web pages.

Preparing Video for the Web

An exciting element of web sites is digital video. You can record digital video for the web with a digital video camera, and then save the video you recorded to your computer using the software provided with your camera. If you don't have a digital video camera, you can pay someone to convert your analog (nondigital) video to digital video.

Many levels of software are available for editing digital video. Recent versions of Microsoft Windows come with the Windows Movie Maker, and newer Macs come with iMovie software. Your digital video camera probably includes editing software as well. Professional movie editors use programs such as Adobe Premiere or Apple's Final Cut Pro to edit video. These programs cost between $500 and $1000, and they provide powerful tools for reducing file size on large videos.

Because digital video files are massive—exponentially larger than regular image files—digital video must be kept small in size and short in duration to make it accessible to visitors to your site. In addition, professional-quality video editing programs include special software that compresses the size of video files. Finally, special programs are available for web site servers (servers that host web sites) that *stream* movies—so that the movies begin to play even before they are fully downloaded.

To watch your videos, visitors must have a *plug-in* viewer—special software that allows them to see the movie. The three most common types of online video players are RealMedia (RM files), QuickTime (MOV files), and Windows Media files (which have a variety of file formats including AVI and MPEG). Movies generated in Flash use the SWF file format, which we'll discuss in a minute.

A discussion of video editing and compression is well beyond the scope of this book, but you can present video at your web site even without using compression software or streaming servers. Following are some guidelines for saving video files for the web:

❏ Keep your video size at 320 pixels wide by 240 pixels high, as shown in Figure 3-10.

Figure 3-10
Saving a movie sized at 320 pixels by 240 pixels, high quality, in Windows Movie Maker

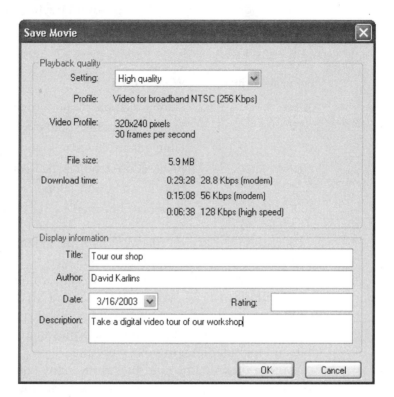

❏ Consider including "best quality," "medium quality," and "low quality" versions of your video, and allow visitors with fast Internet connections to download the best quality, while dial-up visitors can download the low quality version.

❏ Provide links so that visitors can download software to display your video. If you include Real video, provide a link to *www.real.com*. For QuickTime movies, provide a link to *www.quicktime.com*. And for Windows media movies, provide a link to *www.microsoft.com/ windowsmedia/*.

If you plan to include Flash animation in your web site, your visitors will need to have the Flash player plug-in installed with their browser. If they don't have the player, they can download it free from *www.macromedia.com*. Flash files are generally smaller in size than the digital media discussed earlier in this section; therefore, they can be larger in size and longer in length. If you create animation in Flash, you should save it as an SWF file to enable it to be embedded in a web site.

Preparing Sound Files for Your Web Site

You can choose from a multitude of sound file formats to present audio on your web site. The most widely used of these audio file formats are listed and described here:

Audio File Format	What It Does
AIFF	Standard Apple sound format
WAV	Standard Windows sound format
MP3	High quality, low size sound files
RM, RA	RealMedia—requires the RealPlayer
AU	Developed by Sun, supported by many media players
MIDI	A format generated by digital sound software

As with video, sound files require plug-in software on your visitor's computer if he or she is going to hear your web audio. Many free downloadable media plug-ins will play many sound file formats. For example, the RealOne player will play MPEG, WAV, AIFF, AU, and MP3 files, along with Real's own RealMedia sound files. Given the wide availability of plug-in media players, you can fairly safely collect or create sound files in any of the formats listed in the table and include them in your web site.

You can download sound files from many sources. An Internet search will yield long lists of companies that will sell you audio files to use as background sounds for web pages, or you'll find "ring," "click," and "boing" sounds to attach to buttons.

If you want to create a simple audio file from scratch, you can record a file of up to 60 seconds using the free Windows Sound Recorder program. Plug a microphone or other audio input device (such as a cable linking a CD player) into the audio input line on your computer. Launch Sound Recorder (in Windows XP, choose Start | All Programs | Accessories | Entertainment). Click the red Record button, and talk into your microphone or play your sound device. The green line in Sound Recorder will indicate the input volume. Click the black, rectangular Stop button to end the recording:

Choose File | Save to save your audio as a WAV file. You can also use Sound Recorder's Edit menu to cut and paste parts of your sound file to combine with other sound files. The Effects menu provides simple effects—such as Echo and Reverse (that plays sounds backward).

When you save your audio file, sound editing programs allow you to save with different levels of quality, and in stereo or mono. Audio quality depends on sample rates (measured in kilohertz) and bit depth (measured in bits), both of which affect how much data is included in the sound file. Higher quality sound files take longer to download, but they preserve the sound more clearly. Stereo files are about twice as large as similar mono sound files, and they double the download time for your sound file.

Audio files are often compressed to allow them to download faster while retaining more sound quality. Compression methods for both sound and video are called *codecs* (*co*mpression/*dec*ompression). You can choose a codec for your sound file in Windows Sound Recorder by choosing File | Save As, and then clicking the Change button in the Save As dialog box. This opens the Sound Selection dialog box.

The following illustration shows an audio file being saved as an 8,000 kHz, 8-bit Mono file. This sound file requires only about a 7-kilobyte-per-second (kbs) download rate, which will allow visitors with a dial-up connection of 28.8 kbs to hear it without interruption.

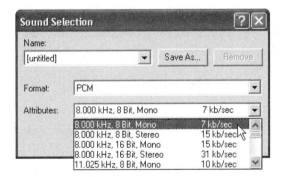

The Format drop-down list in the Sound Selection dialog box allows you to choose from a variety of codec methods. A discussion of audio codec is beyond the scope of this book, but the Windows Media Audio codec is a reliable way to reduce file size while maintaining decent quality audio. The Sonic Spot (*www.sonicspot.com*) is a good source of detailed information on digital audio. You can also easily experiment by saving your audio file using different bit depths and sample rates, and listening to the files as you play them back.

Preparing PDF Files for the Web

The PDF file format allows you to present documents on the web that retain the text formatting and layout of a printed document. Visitors to your web site will need the free, downloadable Adobe Acrobat Reader software to see PDF files at your site. That program can be downloaded from *www.adobe.com/products/acrobat/*.

The Mac OSX operating system allows you to save files as PDF from the Print dialog box of any application. Windows users, however, need additional software to create PDF files. Adobe Acrobat is the most full-featured program available for converting text and image layouts to PDF, but many less costly options are also available. Adobe offers an online service to generate PDF files from Microsoft office files at *http://createpdf.adobe.com*. Free trials are available for this service, and subscriptions are currently about $100 per year for unlimited conversions.

Other free options for converting files to PDF include a free downloadable PDF995 program available at *www.pdf995.com*. This program generates PDF files from your Word document or other files, using a version of a program called GhostScript.

Once you download and install PDF995, you can convert files to PDF files through the File menu. Choose File | Print in your application, and select the PDF995 "printer," as shown in Figure 3-11. This will open a dialog box that will allow you to name the PDF file to which your document is saved.

Figure 3-11
Saving a Word document as a PDF file by printing it to a PDF995 printer file

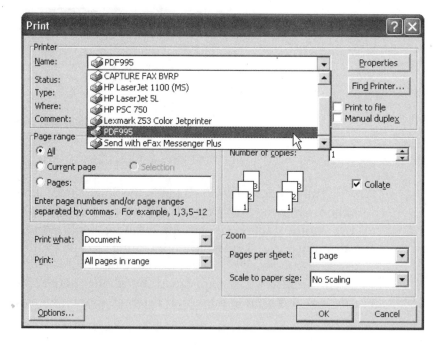

**TESTING
1-2-3**

To ensure smooth sailing as you begin to lay out your web pages, you'll find it worthwhile to go over the following checklist to make sure your web content is ready to use:

❑ Text content should be created, edited, spell-checked, and saved to a text file format. Word files are fine.

❑ Image files should be resized or cropped, if necessary, and saved to GIF or JPEG format.

❑ Video and sound should be saved or converted to a digital format.

❑ Text that must be displayed in fonts other than Arial/Helvetica, Times, or Courier should be saved as graphical text in a graphic file format. Use this technique only for small amounts of text, such as page banners or logos.

❑ Text and graphics documents that must have their formatting preserved closely can be saved as PDF files and integrated into your web site.

In addition to having your web content ready, at this stage of the process you should have arranged for a domain name and web server space. Refer to Chapter 2 for instructions on how to do that.

If you have a domain name and a web server, and your content is ready to go, you can use any of the web design programs covered in the following chapters to lay out your web pages and publish your content to the Internet.

Part II

Creating and Uploading Your Web Site

Chapter 4

Creating Web Pages Using GeoCities PageBuilder

Tools of the Trade

To create a web site with Yahoo! GeoCities PageBuilder, you need only an Internet connection and a computer operating system that supports Java. Because recent versions of Windows and Macintosh operating systems do support Java, you shouldn't need to purchase or download software in advance to create web pages with PageBuilder.

Using PageBuilder is the easiest and most low-cost way to create your web site. You don't need to buy PageBuilder, because it is available with any Yahoo! GeoCities account, including free accounts (although not all options are available for free accounts). The drawbacks to using PageBuilder are that it works only with GeoCities sites, it doesn't have as full a set of features as such programs as FrontPage or Dreamweaver, and once you create your site in PageBuilder, it's difficult (but not impossible) to migrate that site to FrontPage or Dreamweaver later on. If PageBuilder fits your needs, though, you can follow the steps outlined here to create a web site with text, images, links, and other features.

Step 1: Accessing the GeoCities Web Design Tools Online

The simplest path to access PageBuilder is to open a Yahoo! (free) e-mail account. Go to *www.yahoo.com* and click the Email link. If you already have a Yahoo! Mail account, you can simply log in.

If you don't have an e-mail account, click the Sign Up link at the Yahoo! Mail page. This opens the registration form shown in Figure 4-1. Fill out the required areas of the form—Yahoo! ID (username), password, first name, last name, residence, zip, gender, industry, and title. You'll also be prompted to type a word that appears in a graphic (GeoCities uses this field to screen out automated registrations). Finally, click the Submit button at the bottom of the page.

Figure 4-1
The first step in getting logged into PageBuilder is to open a Yahoo! Mail account if you don't already have one.

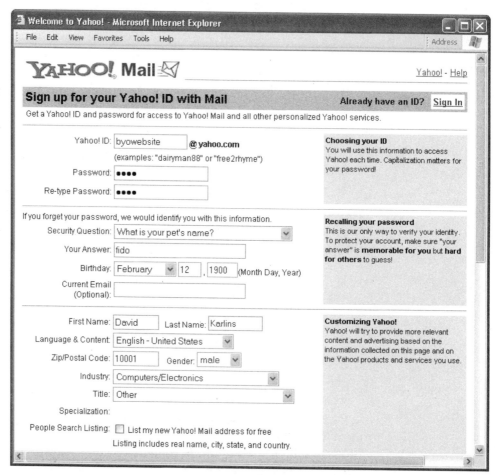

TIPS OF THE TRADE

Avoid Junk Mail Lists

You might want to uncheck the checkboxes in the Mail sign-up form that asks Yahoo! to send you "special offers, promotions, and research surveys from selected Yahoo! partners," and look carefully to make sure you deselect any checkboxes that sign you up for additional junk mail.

After you submit your e-mail sign-up form, you will see a page welcoming you to Yahoo! Mail, and (again) providing you with checkboxes that enroll you in various e-mail junk mail lists. After you select (or deselect) the junk mail options, click the Continue to Yahoo! E-mail button.

Next, you fill in an additional Mail Setup form verifying your first and last name. After you click the Set Me Up button, you'll return to the confirmation page.

Don't Lose Your Password!

Write down the password you assigned yourself, and keep it in a safe place. You'll need this password to log in to your Yahoo! Mail account and to access your web site. If you forget it or lose your password, Yahoo! will assign you a new one if you provided an alternative e-mail account when you signed up, and if you can correctly provide the date of birth information you used when you signed up for your account.

At this point, you have the option of adding Yahoo! to your toolbar, and making Yahoo! Mail your default e-mail program, as shown in Figure 4-2. There is no reason to select this checkbox—you can read your Yahoo! e-mail and create your GeoCities PageBuilder site without it.

Figure 4-2
Deselecting the option
to make Yahoo! Mail
your default e-mail
program

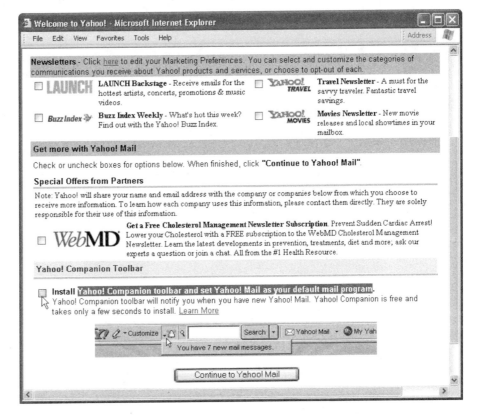

Logging Out...and Logging Back In

You need to be logged into your Yahoo! Mail account to sign up for a GeoCities web site. If for some reason you've logged off, you'll need to log back in to your Yahoo! Mail account to resume the process of signing up for a web site.

While logged into your Yahoo! Mail account, scroll down to the bottom of the Yahoo! Mail page, and click the link to GeoCities, as shown in Figure 4-3.

Figure 4-3
Jumping from
Yahoo! Mail page
to GeoCities

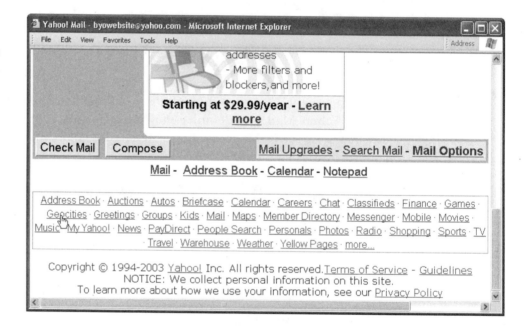

The Yahoo! GeoCities page has links that allow you to sign up for fee-based or free web sites. (Check Chapter 2 for a discussion of how to select a paid site.) Free sites do not support some features (such as the ability to collect data in forms). Using the free service, your site may be inundated with pop-up ads. You can sign up for a free site, as shown in Figure 4-4, and then upgrade to a paid site later, if you need to.

Figure 4-4
Clicking the link to
sign up for a free
GeoCities web site

Find the free →
web site link

Note that if you click the Sign Up Now! link to sign up for a fee-based site, you'll fill out a form in which you can request a domain name, and you'll provide GeoCities with your billing information.

After you click the link to sign up for a free site, you'll be asked what kind of pop-up advertising you want to appear on your web pages. After choosing an ad topic, click the Continue link, as shown in Figure 4-5.

Figure 4-5
Choosing a topic for
ads on a GeoCities
Free site

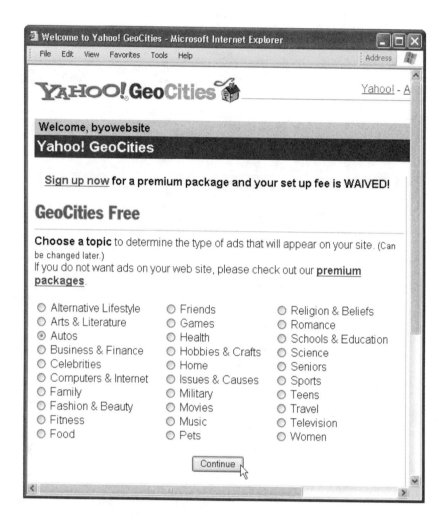

When you've completed the process of signing up for your Yahoo! GeoCities
site for the first time, you'll arrive at the Welcome to GeoCities page that displays
your home page URL (Uniform Resource Locator), as shown in Figure 4-6. This
URL is your new *web site address*. If you've gotten this far, you are now the proud
owner of a web site, and you're ready to add content.

Figure 4-6
At this point, you
have a web site,
and your URL is
displayed.

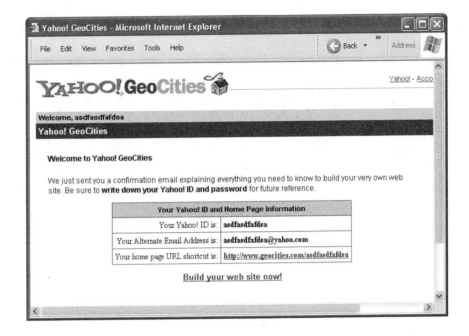

Click the Build Your Web Site Now! link to access the page that allows you to choose a tool for editing your site content. Here, you're offered two options in the Build My Web Site section of the page: Yahoo! PageWizards and Yahoo! PageBuilder. PageWizards are even easier to use than PageBuilder, but they offer little control over your page content and format.

To open PageBuilder, click the Yahoo! PageBuilder link, shown in Figure 4-7.

Figure 4-7
Launching
PageBuilder

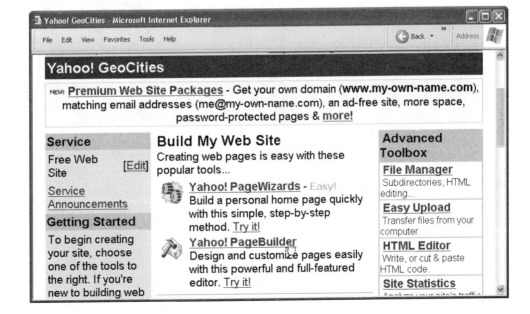

The Yahoo! PageBuilder page provides a short description of the program. Feel free to browse this page. You'll notice that it contains a number of preformatted template pages. After you learn to format and edit pages in PageBuilder, you might want to use one of these templates as a base upon which to build future pages. First, though, you'll need to learn to manage PageBuilder's editing tools.

To start the PageBuilder program, click the Launch PageBuilder link on this page.

If PageBuilder Doesn't Load...

PageBuilder can take several minutes to load, so don't hit the panic button if the program doesn't launch right away. However, if you wait 5 minutes or more, or you see an error message on your computer, or if the Launch PageBuilder link is not visible on your screen, your computer may not currently support the Java programming language that's required for PageBuilder to run on your system. If that's the case, you can click the Install Java link, which will open a page at the Sun Java web site, where you can download Java. For further troubleshooting, find the GeoCities help page link with the text "Turn Java On."

Because PageBuilder is launched online, the exact links required to start the program can change as GeoCities updates its site. Basically, you need to click the appropriate links to launch PageBuilder repeatedly until the small window that says "Yahoo! PageBuilder Loading" opens:

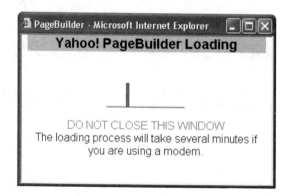

Don't Log Off the Internet While Using PageBuilder

Essential elements of PageBuilder are not downloaded onto your computer. Therefore, you must maintain your Internet connection to GeoCities to use the program. Do not close the small Yahoo! PageBuilder Loading window until you are done with your PageBuilder session.

When PageBuilder finally opens for the first time, you'll see a blank page in the PageBuilder window that looks like the one shown in Figure 4-8. The PageBuilder window has a menu bar, a set of icons for adding page elements (such as text, pictures, and links), and a set of formatting tools that are active only when you have created and selected a block of text.

Figure 4-8
The PageBuilder window opens with a blank page.

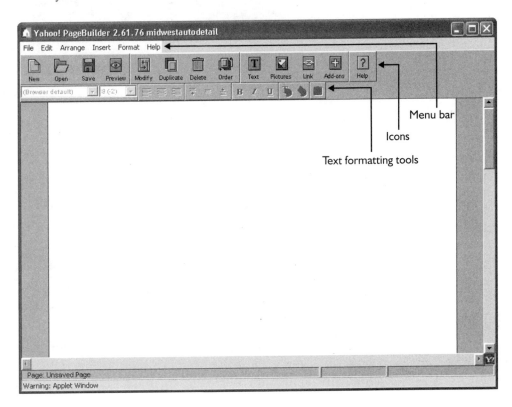

With the blank page open, you're ready to start formatting your page and adding content.

Step 2: Defining Page Properties

The first step in defining your web page properties is to assign a *filename* to your page. Normally, the first page you define in your site is your *home page*—the page that visitors see first when they visit your site. For example, your site might have a dozen web pages, all found at the URL *www.midwestautodetail.com*. Only one of these pages is your home page—the one that opens first after a visitor types *www.midwestautodetail.com* into his or her browser's address bar.

Home pages in PageBuilder are assigned the name *index.html*. You'll want to save your home page with that filename. To do that, click the Save icon. When the Save Page dialog box opens, it will list all the pages in your site. If your site is brand new, the only page available will be the *index.htm* page (it will be listed simply as *index* in the Files Available list). Click index, and then click Save to save your first page as your home page:

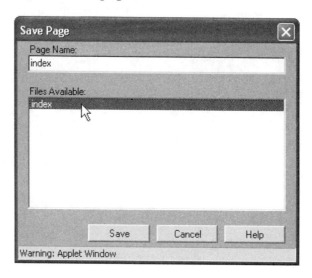

Since you are replacing the generic home page that came with your web site with a new page, you'll be prompted to replace the old page. After you save your page, a Yahoo! PageBuilder dialog box appears asking if you want to view your page in a browser.

Even though the PageBuilder window provides a *close approximation* of what your page will look like, you can't really tell how your page will look to a web visitor until you view it in a web browser. At this point, because you haven't added any content to your page, there isn't much to see. But as you add text, images, formatting, and other elements, you'll want to click OK in this dialog box to see exactly how your page looks in a browser:

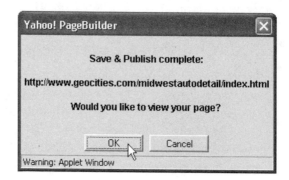

File Naming Rules

Home pages are always named *index*. But other pages can have other file-names. In general, it's safer to avoid using spaces, punctuation, and other special characters (such as %, $, !, and so on) in web page filenames. True, your operating system (Mac or Windows) can handle spaces and special characters in file names. But the web server, the remote computer at Geocities! that will host your web site, does not recognize file names with spaces or special characters.

Now that you've saved your (still blank) home page as *index*, you need to define other page properties. The page *title* is different than the page filename. The title appears in the title bar of a web browser when someone views your page. Page titles can be more descriptive than page names, and they *can* include spaces as well as special characters (such as !, ?, :, or &) that are not advisable in filenames.

To define a page title, choose Format | Page Properties, and enter a page title in the Title area of the Page Properties dialog box.

Keywords help search engines locate your site. They are optional, and current search engine technology does not rely on keywords as much as older search engines did. (Modern search engines rely more on the text content of your page, as well as links to your page from other sites.) If you wish to add keywords, type them in and place commas between them in the Keywords area of the Page Properties dialog box. For example, a web builder for an auto detailing shop in Memphis might enter **auto detail, auto detailing, auto detailing Memphis**.

You'll also want to define your page size. Page size is measured in *pixels* (the tiny dots that make up a monitor display). Most modern computer monitors will display at least 800 pixels in width. However, many web designers choose to restrict page width to a smaller size so that older monitors can display an entire page without site visitors having to use a horizontal scrollbar to navigate from one side of a web page to another. The default page width of 650 in PageBuilder is a safe setting, as is the 1500 pixel page height:

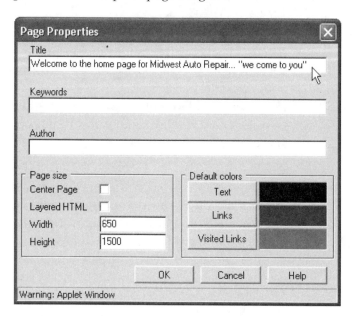

Avoid Overlapping Layers

The Center Page checkbox in the Page Size area of the Page Properties dialog box centers your page in the middle of a visitor's browser window. The Layered HTML checkbox allows you the flexibility of having blocks of text or images overlap each other, but this feature relies on web design tools that are not reliably supported by all web browsers.

By default, PageBuilder will format your text colors so that normal text is black, linked text is blue, and the text in a link that has been visited is red. If you want to change these default colors, click the color swatch for one of the three types of text and choose a different color from the color palette window. Then click OK:

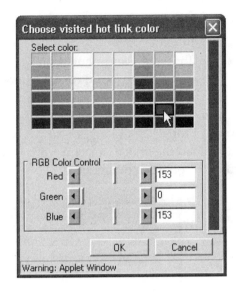

PageBuilder's Colors Are Browser-Safe

The colors in PageBuilder's color palettes are "browser-safe" colors, which means that they can be reliably reproduced in most browsing environments.

You can assign a page background color or page background image to your web page. To change page background color, select File | Background and click the Set Background Color bar in the Background Properties dialog box. Click a color in the Choose Background Color palette, and then click OK:

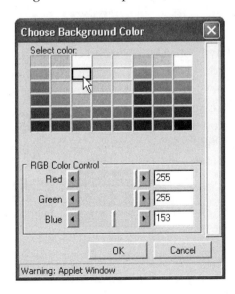

Background images *tile*—that is, they repeat themselves to fill the entire width and height of the page. You can design your own background images or choose one from the wide assortment of background images available from PageBuilder.

To assign a background image, choose Format | Background. If you want to use a background image you've designed or saved on your computer, click [User Files] in the Picture List area, and then click the Upload button in the Background Properties dialog box to navigate to an image you've designed. After you upload the image, select it from your Picture List and click OK in the Background Properties dialog box:

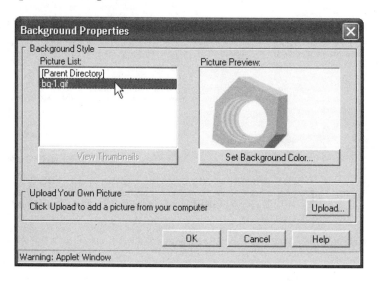

TIPS OF THE TRADE

Using Both a Background Color and a Background Image

You can assign a page background color or a background image, or both. To have both a background color and a tiled background image, set the background color first, and then define a background image. If you use a tiling background image on top of a page background color, you'll want to use a background image that is saved as a GIF file with a transparent background. Or you can simply leave your page background white. It's good to define a background color that matches the dominant color in the tiling background image if you use one, to avoid the color flash that can occur because the background color sometimes downloads faster than the image.

Now that you've defined your page properties, you can begin to create, edit, and format your actual page text content.

Step 3: Creating and Formatting Text

You can't simply type text on the page in PageBuilder, as you can with a word processor program. Before you type in page text, you need to define a text box. You do that by clicking the Text icon. A small, rectangular text box will appear on the page (don't worry; you can move it later). The text box displays four corner handles (small squares) and four side handles. To resize the box, click and drag on any of the handles, as shown in Figure 4-9. When you're resizing a box, the arrow cursor changes to a double arrow, as shown in the figure.

Figure 4-9
Resizing a text box

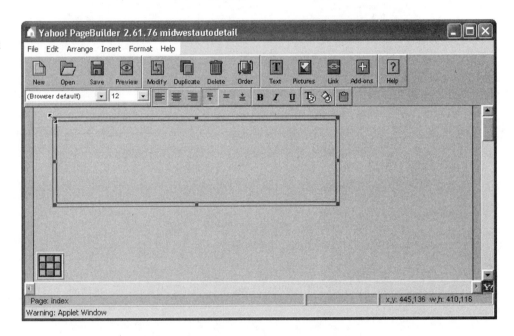

You can also move the text box by clicking and dragging on any point on the box border *except for a sizing handle*. When you're moving a text box, the arrow cursor changes to a four-headed arrow, as shown in Figure 4-10. You can always resize or move your text box again after entering text.

Figure 4-I0
Moving a text box

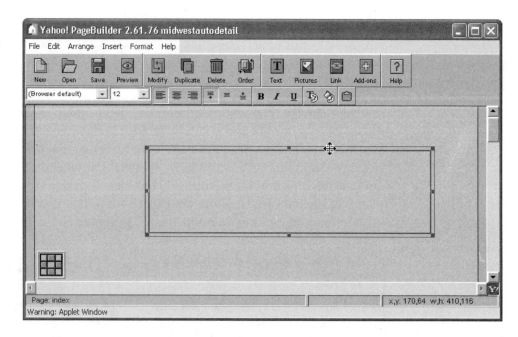

To enter text in a text box, double-click the box and start typing, as shown in Figure 4-11. Most basic word processing editing techniques work in PageBuilder, so you can edit your text any time (after you select the text box).

Figure 4-II
Entering text

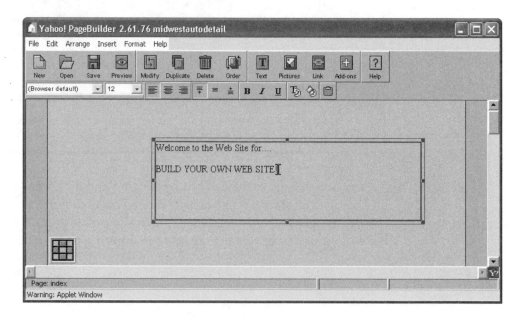

Check Spelling Elsewhere

Unfortunately, PageBuilder does not come with even a rudimentary spell-checking module. For that reason, it's a good idea to create large blocks of text in a word processor first, and then copy and paste them into a PageBuilder text box.

Copying and pasting text into PageBuilder is awkward, but doable. The first step, as with all copying and pasting, is to select text in your word processor, your web browser, or any other program, and then copy it to your operating system clipboard.

With the text copied into the clipboard, switch back to PageBuilder and click the Text tool to create a text box. Resize the text box (or you can do this after you paste your text). With your insertion cursor still inside the text box, click the Clipboard tool to open the PageBuilder Clipboard. Press CTRL-V (COMMAND-V on a Macintosh) to paste the copied (or cut) text into the PageBuilder Clipboard, as shown in Figure 4-12.

Figure 4-12
Pasting copied text into the PageBuilder Clipboard

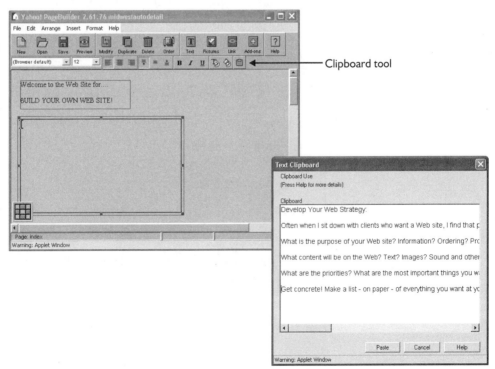

Clipboard tool

TIPS OF THE TRADE

Align Page Objects

You can align several text boxes by selecting them (SHIFT-click to select multiple boxes), and choosing Arrange | Align. The Alignment dialog box has options for aligning objects.

For a visitor to your site to see the fonts you selected to use on your site, the same fonts you used for text must also be installed on the visitor's system. If a visitor's system doesn't include the fonts you used, your visitors will see *different fonts* than the ones you assigned to text. In other words, the visitor's system will replace the fonts you used with fonts available on the visitor's system. Web designers deal with this problem by restricting themselves to a few, widely supported fonts, which are considered "web-safe" fonts: Helvetica/Arial, Times Roman, and Courier (you read about these in Chapter 3). Although these fonts can go by somewhat different names in different systems, almost all systems have installed fonts that closely approximate one of these three font options available in PageBuilder.

To assign a font or font size to an entire box of text, click once on the text box border to select that text box. Alternatively, to assign fonts or font sizes to some of the text within a text box, drag to highlight that text first. With the text box or text selected, choose a font and a font size from the drop-down lists shown in Figure 4-13.

Figure 4-13
Assigning a font size to selected text

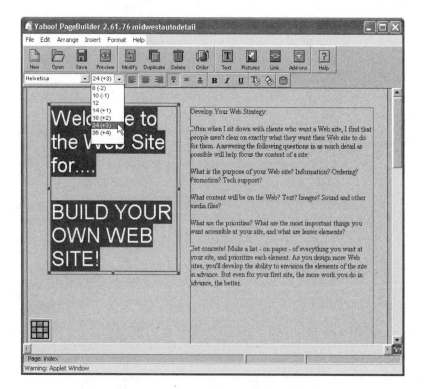

You can left-, right-, or center-align text horizontally in a text box. You can also align text vertically with the top, center, or bottom of a text box. However, you can't select just *some* of the text in a text box and apply horizontal or vertical alignment, because these attributes are assigned to *entire* text boxes. If you need to assign unique alignment to a particular paragraph, that paragraph needs to be in its own text box.

To align text within a text box, select the text box and click one of the horizontal or vertical alignment options, as shown in Figure 4-14.

Figure 4-14
Aligning text
in a text box

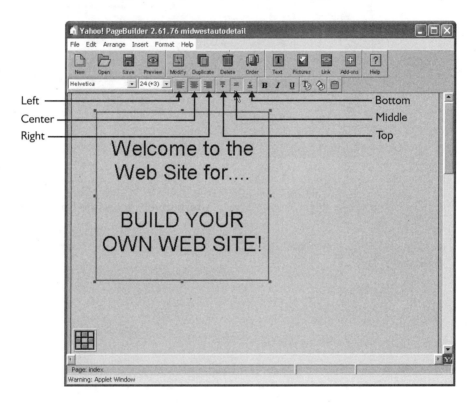

To assign boldface, italics, or underlining to any selected text, highlight the text in a text box, and then click the Boldface, Italic, or Underline button, as shown in Figure 4-15. While it's technically possible to underline text, in general you should avoid doing that because many web viewers will associate underlined text with a link.

Figure 4-I5
Assigning boldface

You can assign background colors to text boxes, or you can assign colors to the text itself. To assign color to some text within the box, highlight the text and click the Choose Text Color tool. Then select a color from the Choose Text Color palette and click OK.

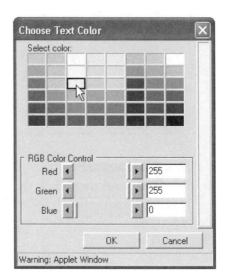

Step 4: Embedding Images

In Chapter 3, you learned to prepare images from digital cameras, scanners, and graphic design software for the web by saving them as JPEG or GIF images. You can easily embed these images on your page in PageBulder. You can also use PageBuilder's online set of clip art and photos as a source of images.

To place a picture on your page, click the Pictures icon to open the Select Picture dialog box.

To insert clip art or one of the photos available from PageBuilder's artwork, double-click [clipart] in the Picture List area of the dialog box. This reveals a set of online folders with different categories of clip art. To view the photos in any category, double-click that category. As you click an image in the list, you can preview it in the Picture Preview area, as shown next. Click OK to insert the picture on your page.

To upload an image from your computer, click the Upload button in the Select Picture dialog box. In the Upload Image dialog box that opens, click Browse and navigate through your computer's file directories to locate the image you will be uploading. Double-click the image file, and then click Upload in the Upload

Image dialog box shown next. This transfers a copy of the selected image from your computer to your remote GeoCities web site.

When you have uploaded your picture, click OK to place it on your page. You can move images on your page the same way you move text boxes—by simply dragging the image, as shown in Figure 4-16. You can resize an image by clicking on a side or corner handle of a selected image and dragging in to shrink or out to enlarge the image.

Figure 4-16
Moving an image
into place

TIPS OF THE TRADE

Try Not to Enlarge Images in PageBuilder

Enlarging images can make them grainy and blurry. Shrinking them does not degrade image quality, but it also doesn't save on file size or download time, because the properties of the original image are still saved as part of the image file. In general, you should size images *before* you start working on them in PageBuilder. If you do resize images in PageBuilder, click and drag from a corner handle, not the side handle, to retain the original height-to-width ratio.

You can also assign links, screen tips, and mouse-over pictures to your images in the Select Picture dialog box. To edit these attributes for an existing picture on your page, double-click the image to open the dialog box.

Screen tips are text messages that appear when a visitor hovers the mouse over an image. These text messages are referred to as *Alt* (alternative) *text* in web design, and they are also used by reading software for web surfers who are sight impaired (the reader software reads the Alt text out loud). Finally, some browsers do not display images, and the Alt text displays instead. Enter the Alt text you want to appear in your web page in the Screen Tip field of the Select Picture dialog box.

A *mouse-over picture* (also called a *rollover*) changes the displayed image when a visitor moves the mouse over the image. This makes your page more interactive and dynamic. The mouse-over picture should be the same size as the original image, or else the second image will distort to fit into the size of the original picture. Assign a mouse-over picture by clicking the Choose button to the right of the Mouse-Over Picture field in the Select Picture dialog box; then either upload an image from your computer, or choose from the clip art and photo gallery. See Figure 4-17.

Step 5: Defining Links for Pictures and Text

Links are one of the most basic and dynamic elements of a web site. Well-placed
links help visitors navigate around your site, and they enable visitors to jump
easily to other online resources. Images or text can be assigned link properties.

Links can be clicked to open a new web page, either at your site or at another
location on the web. Clicking a link can also open a file, such as an image file, a
sound file, or a video file. Clicking an e-mail link launches a visitor's e-mail program with a selected e-mail address in the To: area of the message.

You can assign a link to either selected text or a selected image by clicking the
Link icon. This opens the Hot Link dialog box, shown next. Use the drop-down
menu to choose the kind of link you are defining. If you are linking to a location
outside your web site (such as another web site), choose the Web URL option. If
you are linking to a page in your site, choose the My Page option. If you are linking to an e-mail address, choose E-Mail from the list. If you are linking to a file at
your site that is not a web page (such as an image, a PDF file, or any other file that
is not a web page), choose the My File option.

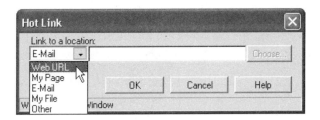

If you are defining a link to a web URL, you can copy and paste the URL from a text file or from the address bar of your browser. If you are using the My Page or My File option to link to a page or file in your site, click the Choose button to select the link target. If you are linking to an e-mail address, enter the e-mail address in the dialog box, like so:

Another way to assign a link to an image is to double-click the image and define the link in the Link To A Location area of the Select Picture dialog box.

More complex web design programs allow you to define whether you want a link to open in the same browser window or in a new browser window. A limitation of PageBuilder is that links defined in the Hot Link dialog box open in the same browser window.

Step 6: Generating JavaScript for Interactivity and Animation

You can make your web site more dynamic and fun by including elements that move around on your page—either on their own or in response to something a visitor does.

To access PageBuilder's animated effects, click the Add-ons icon, and select Page Effects in the Categories list. The IE Page Transitions effect adds changeover effects such as blend or wipe when a visitor enters or leaves your web page. The text and image trail effects allow you to assign an image or text that will trail behind a visitor's cursor. Other effects cause images to move around on your page.

Each page effect, such as the text tail effect, has its own dialog box, where you define parameters such as what image or text is displayed, and how:

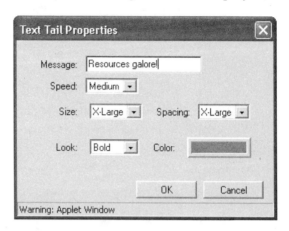

Your page effects won't display in PageBuilder; you'll need to open your page in a web browser to see how they work, as you can see in Figure 4-18. After you define a page effect, you can test it by saving your page and then clicking OK when prompted "Would you like to view your page?" in the PageBuilder (Save) dialog box.

Figure 4-18
Testing an effect in a browser

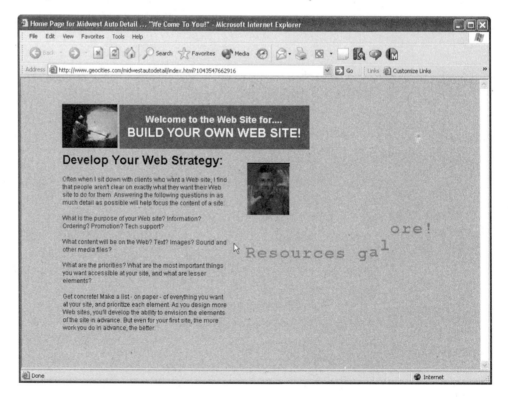

Each page effect is indicated in PageBuilder by an icon on the bottom of the screen, as shown in Figure 4-19. You can remove a page effect by selecting the effect icon and pressing the DELETE key. Or you can double-click an icon to open the dialog box for the selected page effect and edit the settings.

Figure 4-19
Delete page effect icons to delete an effect

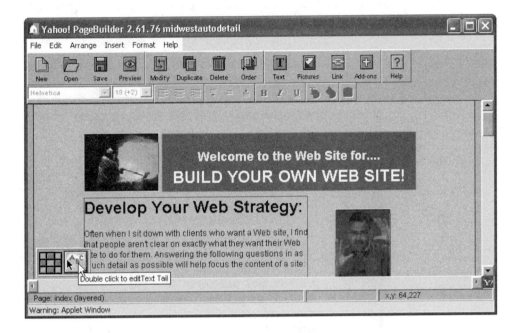

Most of GeoCities' page effects are a bit too distracting and goofy for professional sites, but they have limited usefulness in entertainment or youth-oriented sites.

Step 7: Including Media in Your PageBuilder Site

You can upload sound or video files to your site and let visitors play those media files by clicking a link to the file. Or you can assign a background sound to a page that plays automatically when a visitor comes to your page.

You can download sound and video files from many sources on the Internet (search for *free downloadable sound files* or *free downloadable video clips*). You can also create your own sound file (for instance, your voice welcoming people to your site).

If you want to use an audio file as a page background sound, PageBuilder currently supports MIDI and WAV sound files. Look for (or create) a sound file in one of those two formats if you're using it as a page background. For an explanation of how to create sound files, refer back to the section "Preparing Sound Files for Your Web Site" in Chapter 3.

After you've downloaded or created a sound or video file, use the following instructions to associate it with your site.

Sound or media files that you include in your PageBuilder site will open in a separate browser window, using whatever sound or video player your visitor's system is configured to launch to play media. It's often helpful to include a link on your site so that visitors can download the Real player (from *www.real.com*), the QuickTime player (from *www.quicktime.com*), or the Windows Media Player (*www.microsoft.com/windows/windowsmedia/*). Figure 4-20 shows an example of how you can point visitors to the appropriate player.

Figure 4-20
Providing a link for visitors to download the QuickTime player

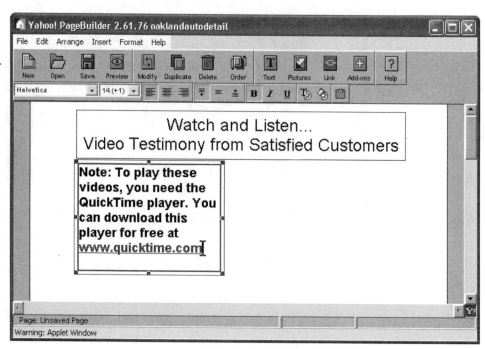

Here's how to upload a media file in PageBuilder:

1. Choose File | Upload Files and Images. The Upload Files dialog box opens.

2. Click the first Browse button and navigate to the media file you want to upload on your computer, as shown in Figure 4-21. You can upload as many as five files at a time. After you have selected all the media files you want to upload, click Upload.

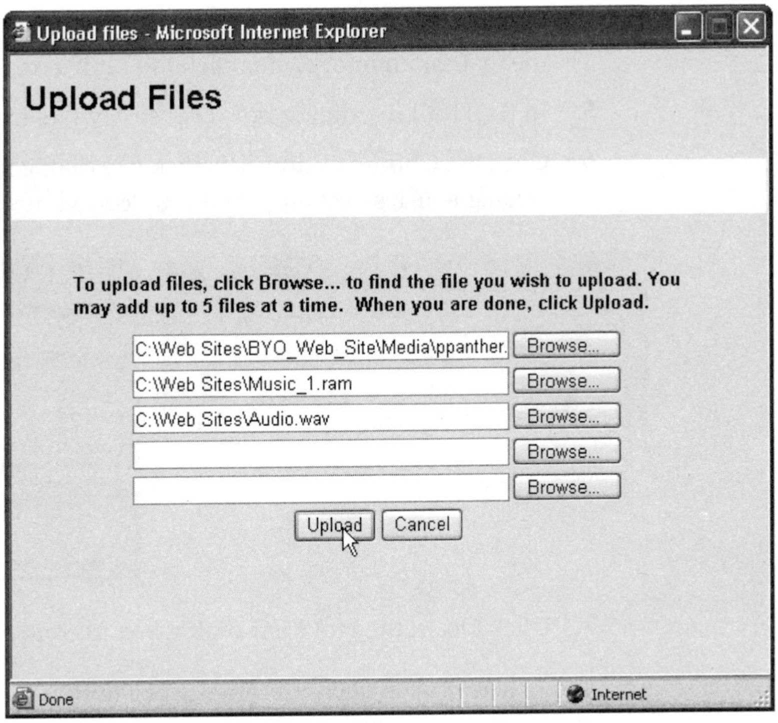

Figure 4-21
Uploading media
files for your site

3. When all the files are uploaded, you'll see a confirmation box. You can now link to your audio and video files. To place a link on your page to an audio or video file, place some text or an image on your page that will serve as the link to the file, as you can see in Figure 4-22.

Figure 4-22
Creating text and
images to link to
media files

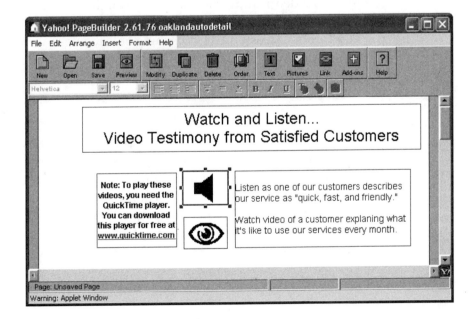

4. Finally, it's time to link your text and/or images(s) to media files. Select the text, or an image, and click the Link icon.

5. In the Hot Link dialog box, choose My File from the drop-down list.

6. Click the Choose button. The Pick File dialog box opens. From the Files Available list, select one of your uploaded media files, and then click OK.

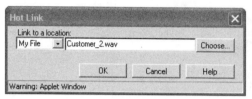
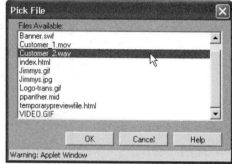

7. Click OK in the Hot Link dialog box to complete the linking process.

Now, when a visitor clicks the link, he or she will open the audio or video file in a separate window, using the media player software installed on the user's system.

TIPS OF THE TRADE

Large Videos Take Time to Download

If your video or audio file is large, you might want to include a warning on your web page that the file will take some time to download. If your visitors are not accustomed to watching or listening to web media, you might also include an explanation that the audio or video file will open in their own media software on their computer.

Linking to an audio or video file is pretty straightforward, and—as emphasized—simply launches the audio or video file in the visitor's own software, as you can see in Figure 4-23. Embedding an audio file as a background sound is a little different, however. Visitors will not consciously launch the sound file; it will play automatically when the page is opened.

Figure 4-23
Launching an audio
file from a link

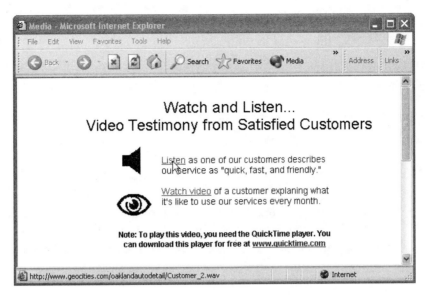

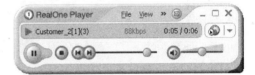

1. To embed a sound file on a page, choose Insert | Basics | Background
   Music. This launches the Background Sound Properties dialog box. Use
   the Choose button in the dialog box to navigate to a sound file.

2. Select a sound file in the Pick File dialog box and click OK.

3. Click the Loop checkbox in the Background Sound Properties dialog
   box if you want your page background sound to repeat indefinitely
   (until a visitor leaves the page).

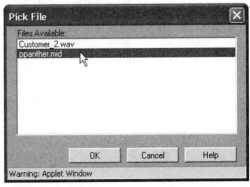

4. Then click OK in the Background Sound Properties dialog box to add the sound to your page.

No Sound Files Listed?

If no sound files are listed in the Pick File dialog box, that means you haven't successfully uploaded a sound file in either the MIDI (.mid) or WAV (.wav) file format. Remember, only MIDI or WAV files can be used as page background sounds.

To edit the background sound properties, double-click the background sound icon that appears on your page (it won't be visible in visitor's browsers), as you can see in Figure 4-24. You can remove the background sound by clicking the background sound icon and pressing DELETE.

Figure 4-24
Edit or delete a background sound using the Background Sound icon.

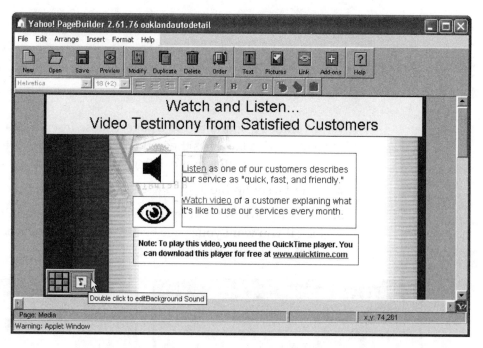

Step 8: Adding Yahoo! and GeoCities Content to Your Site

PageBuilder allows you to insert "Instant Info" onto your pages. Instant Info is updated with interactive content supplied by Yahoo! and GeoCities. Instant Info includes a date and time stamp that tells visitors the current date and time, search boxes linked to Yahoo! or GeoCities' search engines, a counter, and links to Yahoo! maps or directions, stock quotes, and weather.

To insert any of these features, choose Insert | Instant Info, and then choose one of the available features. Click and drag to move the element to a location on your page. Much of the content of the Instant Info features is embedded in your site from the Yahoo! server, so you won't be able to see the actual content in PageBuilder; you'll see markers for the content instead, as shown in Figure 4-25.

Figure 4-25
Placing Instant Info in PageBuilder

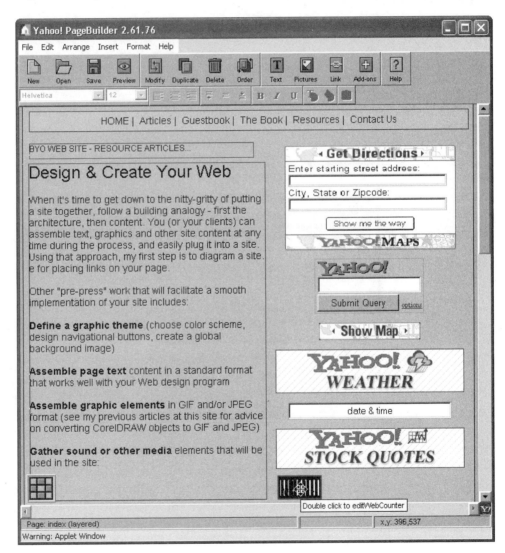

Double-click any of these markers to edit the settings for your Instant Info, or click and delete a marker to remove that element.

To see how your Instant Info elements will look in a browser, save your page and click OK when prompted with "Do you want to see your page?" The embedded content will be updated based on material at Yahoo!, and your page may look like the one shown in Figure 4-26.

Figure 4-26
Testing your instant content in a browser

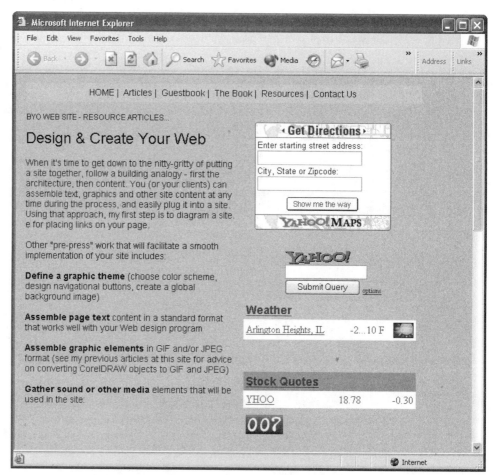

You can also insert news updates from different parts of the world or news on different topics. These news headlines provide links to coverage from Reuters, AP, and other news sources. Insert news headlines by selecting Insert | Headings, and choosing a topic or region. After you select a topic or region, a Properties dialog box appears, where you can define the source of information, the number of headlines, and formatting features:

As with Instant Info elements, you need to save your site and view it (or click the Preview icon) to see the actual content.

For kids' sites, PageBuilder also allows you to insert links to Yahooligans web pages.

Step 9: Managing Your Site

After you've created web pages, you can view and manage the files that have been uploaded to the remote GeoCities server by selecting File | FileManager. This opens the FileManager window for your site.

You can use the FileManager window to upload a file from your computer, to copy or move a file between file folders on your site, or to delete, rename, or duplicate a file. The Refresh button updates the FileManager window to show recently uploaded files.

When you want to copy, move, rename, delete, or duplicate a file, click the checkbox for that file and choose an option from the icons at the top of the FileManager window. For instance, to rename a file, click the file's checkbox, and then click Rename. A dialog box will open, where you can change the name of the file.

The four tabs across the top of the FileManager window allow you to see your pages, images, other files (like media files), and all files in the window, as shown in Figure 4-27.

Figure 4-27
Using the
FileManager
window

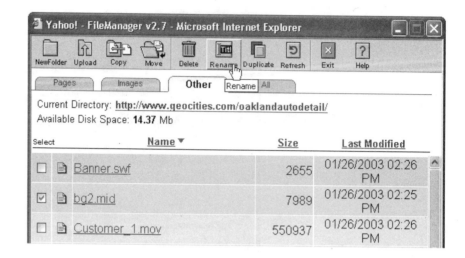

Step 10: Adding Resources

In addition to features available in PageBuilder, you can add additional features to your site by using available online resources, such as mailing lists and search boxes.

The next two chapters in this book explore building web sites in FrontPage (Chapter 5) and Dreamweaver (Chapter 6). Feel free to look over those chapters to learn about more advanced features available in those programs that allow more control over page formatting. Or, feel free to skip to Chapter 7, where you'll learn to add input forms to build a managed, online mailing list; to create an interactive guestbook; and to add other features such as a search box for your site.

**TESTING
1-2-3**

The essential element in creating and posting web pages with PageBuilder is that your internet connection is maintained constantly while you work on your pages:

❑ You'll want a reliable web connection. If you are connected to the Internet through a dial-up connection, consider upgrading to DSL before using PageBuilder. That will reduce the time it takes for PageBuilder to launch each session, and provide you with a more reliable connection.

❑ The best way to protect against your work being lost, or not uploaded, is to *save your page frequently.* By saving frequently, and previewing your pages as you change them, you'll integrate testing into the process of creating your pages, and minimize the damage that can occur if your Internet connection drops while working on your site.

Chapter 5

Creating Web Pages with FrontPage

For the steps in this chapter, you'll need to have Microsoft FrontPage in-stalled and be connected to the Internet in order to access the sign-up pages for various search engines and directories. FrontPage (except for the very first edition) is not available for Macs, only for Windows. Also, very impor-tant: If you plan to publish your FrontPage web page to a server, make sure your server supports FrontPage extensions (for a full explanation of server features and options, refer to the section "Buying Server Space" in Chapter 2). The steps and illustrations in this section are based on FrontPage 2002 but will work with minor adjustments in other versions of FrontPage.

Even before you begin to design your site in FrontPage, you'll want to organize your site content. If you carefully followed the steps outlined in Chapter 3 for organizing your text, images, and media files *before* you start putting your site together, the process of creating your web pages in FrontPage will be much simpler.

Like Dreamweaver and other web site design programs, FrontPage will ask you to specify a root folder (called a *root web* in FrontPage). This is the folder that contains the files you want to include in your site. So, organize your files in a folder on your hard drive before you even start to crank up FrontPage.

In Chapter 2, you learned how to arrange for server space for your web site from a web hosting company. If you're going to be using FrontPage, you'll want to make sure your site provider supports FrontPage *extensions* files that make it easier for FrontPage to connect with your server.

If you've got login information from your web host provider and your files are organized, you're ready to start FrontPage.

What if You Don't Have a Web Server Yet?

You can design a web site on your local drive with FrontPage and upload (FrontPage uses the term publish) the content to a web server later. There are some features in FrontPage web pages that cannot be tested until your site has been published to a web server with FrontPage extensions.

Step 1: Define Your FrontPage Web

The first step in working with FrontPage is to tell the program where your existing files are organized. Do that by following these steps:

1. Start FrontPage.

2. Choose File | New Page or Web. The New Page or Web Task Pane opens.

3. Click the Empty Web link in the Task Pane on the right side of the FrontPage window, as shown in Figure 5-1. (If the Task Pane isn't visible, choose View | Task Pane to display it). The Web Site Templates dialog box opens, with Empty Web selected.

Figure 5-1
Starting to create a
new FrontPage Web

If You Don't See an Empty Web Link...

If your version of FrontPage does not display the Empty Web link in the Task Pane, you can choose Web Site Templates in the Web Site Templates dialog box to access a list of templates. Choose Empty Web and click OK.

4. In the Web Site Templates dialog box, click the Browse button.

5. Use the New Web Location dialog box to navigate to the folder where you stashed the files you'll be using in your web site.

6. After you navigate to the folder containing your files, click the Open button in the New Web Location dialog box. Your file location will appear in the Specify The Location Of The New Web field, as shown in Figure 5-2.

Figure 5-2
Defining the home folder for your FrontPage Web

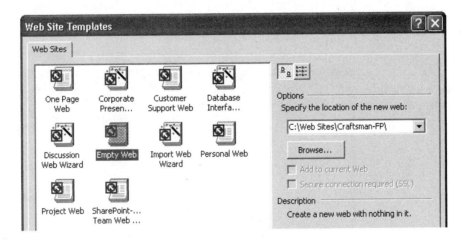

7. Click OK in the Web Site Templates dialog box to finish defining your web site.

Next time you want to work on this web site, choose File | Open Web Sites, and navigate to your *web* (folder) in the Open Web dialog box. Once you navigate to the FrontPage web, click Open to open that web. You can close a FrontPage web by choosing File | Close Web.

Step 2: Manage Your FrontPage Web in Folders View

The Views bar on the left side of the FrontPage window allows you to move among various views of your web site. The two most important views are Page view, where you edit and format your web pages, and Folders view, where you can look at and manage your site files.

View your site by clicking the Folders icon in the Views bar. If your Views bar is hidden, choose View | Views Bar to active it.

As soon as you look at your site in Folders view, you'll see that FrontPage has created two folders, _private and Images. The _private folder is used for data submitted by input forms that use FrontPage extensions to manage form data input. These features require a web site with FrontPage extensions, and are beyond the scope of this book. FrontPage extensions generally duplicate the features available from CGI scripts, which are explored in Chapter 7. The Images folder is available for you to save image files.

You can open, cut, copy, rename, or delete any file in your web by right-clicking that file and choosing a feature from the context menu. Figure 5-3 shows a file being renamed. You can move files from one folder to another by clicking and dragging in Folders view.

Figure 5-3
Renaming a file
in Folders view

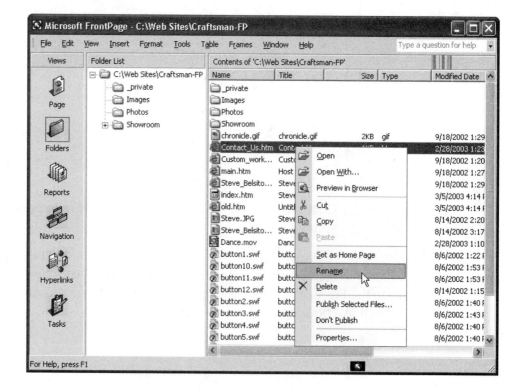

Do File Management in FrontPage!

If you rename, copy, or move a file in Folders view, FrontPage will make adjustments in your pages to update links between pages, or links to pictures embedded in your pages. If you do your file management outside of FrontPage (using the Windows Explorer program, for example), you'll corrupt (break) links between files. So, do your file management in FrontPage, using Folders view.

Step 3: Edit Pages in Page View

Editing and formatting text and images in FrontPage's Page view is very similar to other Microsoft Office programs like Word, Publisher, or PowerPoint. If you've used those programs, you've got a good start on creating and editing page content.

You can switch to Page view by clicking on the Page icon in the Views bar. Or, you can open an HTML file in Page view by double-clicking it. To enter text in Page view, just type as you would in Word.

1. Once you've entered (or pasted) text into a FrontPage web page, basic Microsoft Office editing tools like cut, copy, and paste work just as they do in Word, as do Edit | Find and Edit | Replace.

2. Use the Standard toolbar in Page view to manage most page editing tasks. The New button can create many new things—pages, webs, even task lists. The Standard toolbar is illustrated in Figure 5-4.

Figure 5-4
Many editing tools are on the Standard toolbar.

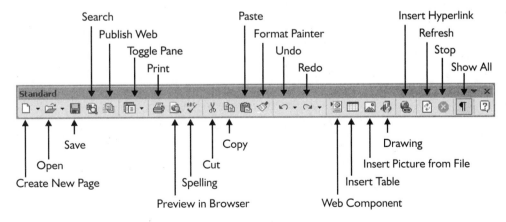

Many of these Standard toolbar options work just as they do with other Office applications—Cut, Copy, Paste, and Save are self-explanatory. Other

FrontPage tools look like buttons you're familiar with in Office applications, but work a little differently.

The Open button is a drop-down menu that enables you to open either pages or webs. The Create New Page drop-down list enables you to create a new page, web site, task, folder, a document library, list, or survey (these last three are used for intranets on special Microsoft web servers). The Search button opens search pane that can be used to find files in your web site (just use Edit | Find if you're looking for text on your open web page).

The Publish Web button uploads your site files to a web server. You'll learn to do that at the end of this chapter. The Toggle Pane button displays or hides the panes on the right side of the FrontPage window. The Print button prints your web page. The Preview in Browser button displays your page in a browser.

The Web Component button opens the Insert Web Component dialog box features like Java buttons (animated buttons), search boxes, and hit counters. These features require FrontPage extensions, and if they are grayed out in the Insert Web Component dialog box, your server doesn't support them. Figure 5-5 shows the Insert Web Component dialog box, with a few features grayed out.

Figure 5-5
Features in the Web Component dialog box require that your site is published to a server with FrontPage extensions.

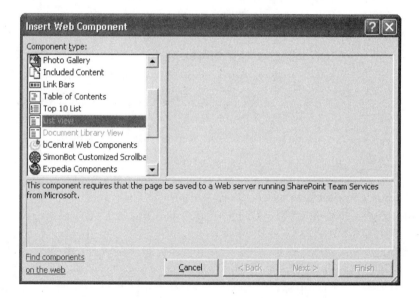

The Insert Picture from File button opens the Picture dialog box, and lets you find a picture to place on your page. The Drawing button displays the Drawing toolbar, but illustrations created with the Drawing toolbar are not reliably supported in web pages and should be avoided.

You'll use the Insert Hyperlink button to define a link for selected text or a selected picture. The Refresh button reverts your page to the last saved version. The Stop button breaks the connection between a page and a remote server.

The Show All button displays formatting elements like line breaks and paragraph marks.

Some of these buttons are shortcuts for menu features that you'll learn in the course of this chapter. Others are standard formatting and editing tools that you can use to edit text.

Step 4: Format Text

Even more than the Standard toolbar, FrontPage's Formatting toolbar will look familiar to users of Microsoft Office programs.

What's the same? The Bold, Italic, and Underline buttons do what you would expect (but web designers avoid using underlining since it is generally associated with link text). The Align Left, Center, Align Right, and Justify buttons define paragraph alignment. The Numbering and Bullets buttons apply automatic numbering or bullet formatting to selected paragraphs. The Increase Indent and Decrease Indent buttons move selected paragraph margins in or out. The Highlight Color button applies a background color to selected text. The Font Color button applies color to selected text.

What's different in the Formatting toolbar? The Styles drop-down list offers a *limited* set of web compatible styles, as opposed to the more flexible and easily definable styles in Microsoft Word. The Font Size drop-down menu, shown next, offers seven sizes of text that are compatible with web browsers.

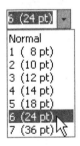

What's Normal?

The "Normal" option in the Font Size drop-down list matches font size to the HTML style you select in the Style drop-down list on the Formatting toolbar. This option is useful to designers using predefined HTML styles but not relevant if you are just assigning font sizes to selected text, as you are doing here.

You can use the Font drop-down list to select from a full set of fonts. However, font display in web pages is dependent on the fonts on your *visitor's* computer. So, web designers usually restrict themselves to Arial, Times Roman, and Courier, which are supported in almost every operating system. If you choose other fonts, a visitors operating system might substitute a different font, disrupting your page layout.

The color palette that appears when you click the Font Color button and choose More Colors are web-compatible, as shown next. That means they are supported reliably by most operating systems and browsers. Stick to these colors to ensure that your text color stays consistent for all your visitors.

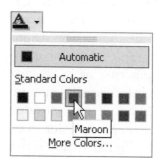

Step 5: Format Paragraphs

You can define paragraph formatting features like line spacing, indenting, and even borders and shading in FrontPage. Other paragraph formatting features include line numbering or bullets, or aligning paragraphs using the Align Left, Center, Align Right, or Justify buttons.

In addition to the paragraph formatting available using the buttons in the Formatting toolbar, you can define more paragraph attributes to selected text in the Paragraph dialog box. To do that, follow these steps (with your paragraph selected).

1. Select Format | Paragraph.

2. Define indentation before text (on the left), after text (on the right), or to the first line only in the Indentation fields of the dialog box.

3. Assign vertical spacing by entering values in the Before or After boxes.

4. Define word spacing by entering values in the Word box. In the Line Spacing drop-down menu, the options are for single spacing, double spacing, or halfway in between.

After you define paragraph properties in the Paragraph dialog box, as shown in Figure 5-6, click OK.

Figure 5-6
Defining paragraph
formatting

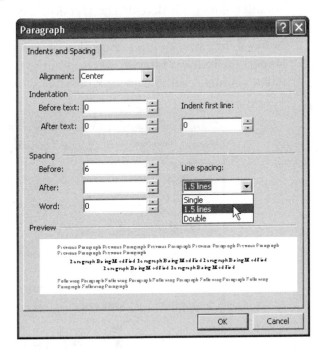

Step 6: Format Page Properties

Page properties include page background color (or *tiling*—repeating background image), background sound, page margins, and default colors for your page text, links, and page title. To define page properties for an open page, choose File | Properties, which opens the Page Properties dialog box.

Page Properties Are Controlled by Themes

FrontPage has a feature called "themes" that assigns a set of formatting attributes to all the pages in your site. Themes restrict the formatting you can apply on your own, and generally make your web site more difficult to edit in HTML or migrate to other web design software. For those reasons, this chapter will not address or encourage the use of themes. To learn to use themes Styles, and other features of FrontPage not covered in this book, check out FrontPage 2002 Virtual Classroom (McGraw-Hill/Osborne, 2001), by David Karlins.

Use the Background tab in the Page Properties dialog box to define page background and default text colors, as shown in Figure 5-7. You can also define default colors for link text. The Hyperlink color box defines the color of unvisited links. The Visited Hyperlinks box defines the color of visited links, and the Active Links box defines the color of links being clicked. Select the Enable Hyperlink Rollover Effects Use checkbox to define a font format that will display when visitors scroll over a link on your page.

Figure 5-7
Setting a page background color, and default text and link colors

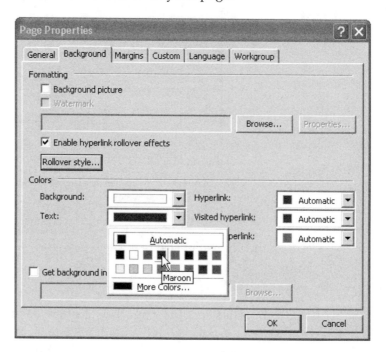

TIPS OF THE TRADE

Default Text Colors and Defined Text Colors

Text formatting that you apply to selected text on a page *takes precedence over* default text colors defined in the Page Properties dialog box. For example, if you set the default page text as *gray* but assign *red* to selected text, the color you define on the page itself will override the default page color.

You can *tile* (repeat) an image across your page as a page background by clicking the Browse button in the Background tab of the Page Properties dialog box. Navigate to an image file in the Set Background Picture dialog box, and click Open to select an image. When you click OK in the dialog box, the selected image becomes the page background. The Get Background And Colors From Page checkbox enables you to define background and text colors on your page based on another page.

After you define page background properties, click OK to close the Page Properties dialog box and to apply the selected options to your page.

Step 7: Add a Background Sound to Your Page

Page background sounds play when your page is opened. Background sound can play just once or over and over. Sound files tend to be large and can severely increase the time it takes for a web page to download. Not everyone appreciates hearing sound files when they open a web page, but if you think your visitors will appreciate a background sound, FrontPage makes it easy to include one.

To add background sounds to your page, click the General tab in the Page Properties dialog box and follow these steps:

1. Click the Browse button to navigate to a sound file in the Background Sound dialog box.

2. Select the file and click Open. Your selected file appears in the Location box in the General tab of the Page Properties dialog box.

3. To repeat the sound endlessly, select the Forever checkbox. Or, deselect the Forever checkbox and set the number of times the sound will play by entering a value in the Loop box.

4. Click OK to close the Page Properties dialog box and then save your page.

Background Sound File Formats Can Be...

File formats supported for page background sounds in FrontPage 2002 are WAV, MID or MIDI, RAM or RA, AIF, AU, and SND. Use sound files of these formats as a background sound for your page.

Step 8: Define Page Margins

Typically, browsers insert a small space on the top and left side of web pages. You can remove that margin by following these steps:

1. With your web page open, select File | Properties.

2. Select the Margins tab of the Page Properties dialog box, and check both checkboxes in the dialog box.

3.   Enter 0 (zero) in the Top and Left margin checkboxes, as shown here.

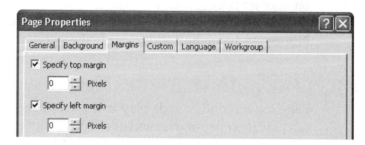

4.   Click OK to close the dialog box and to apply the new margins.

Step 9: Define Keywords and Page Descriptions

Keywords are used by search engines to list your site. Page descriptions provide a summary of your site that is also used by search engines when they list your site. Figure 5-8 shows a site description in a results list from the Google search engine. This description is based on the page description assigned to that page.

Figure 5-8
A page description appears when a site is listed by a search engine.

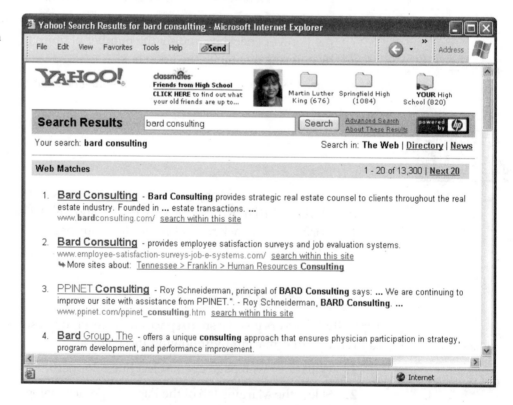

Keyword Advice

In Chapter 8, you'll learn more about how to use keywords and other elements to optimize your listing in search engines.

To assign keywords and descriptions for an open page, select File | Properties to open the Page Properties dialog box. Click the Custom tab in the dialog box, and click the Add button in the User Variables area of the dialog box.

To define a list of keywords, enter **Keywords** in the Name box of the User Meta Variable dialog box. Enter a list of words or phrases separated by commas in the Value box, as shown here:

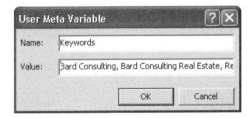

These words or phrases should be text that you anticipate people will type into a search box when they are looking for your site. Click OK to close the User Meta Variable dialog box after you enter keywords.

To define a description for your site, click the Add button in the User Variables area of the dialog box again. Enter **Description** in the Name box of the User Meta Variable dialog box. Enter a description for your site in the Value box, as shown here:

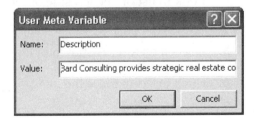

Step 10: Add Pictures

In Chapter 3, you learned that it's important to prepare images *before* you begin to design your web site. Only images in GIF, JPEG, or PNG format are consistently recognized by web browsers without additional plug-in software.

If you're working with FrontPage, you can break that rule—kind of. FrontPage will take images in many different file formats including TIFF (often used for scanned images) or BMP (Windows bitmap), and automatically convert them to GIF or JPEG images.

In addition, you can even copy and paste images from many file formats into FrontPage. Essentially, if you can see a picture on your screen in Windows, you can copy and paste it into FrontPage.

Avoid FrontPage Drawing Tools

FrontPage also has a toolbar with drawing tools. However, the pictures generated by these tools are done so in VML format, a format that is not reliably supported in web browsers and should be avoided. Also, avoid copying and pasting drawings that you create in Word, PowerPoint, and other Office applications into FrontPage; they too are in VML format.

To insert a GIF, JPEG, or PNG image into a page, follow these steps:

1. Place your cursor insertion point where you want to insert the picture.

2. Choose Insert | Picture | From File. The Picture dialog box opens.

3. In the Picture dialog box, choose one of the sources for files from the Look In list on the left side of the dialog box.

4. Navigate to the folder with your picture file.

5. Select a picture, as shown in Figure 5-9.

6. Click Insert to place the image in your web page.

Figure 5-9
Selecting an
image to insert

Step 11: Resize Images

As you learned in Chapter 2, you can enlarge images in FrontPage, but when you do you'll distort the image because the total number of *pixels* (dots) won't change. So, you'll want to avoid enlarging images in FrontPage. You can, however, reduce file size.

To change the size of an image, select it and then click and drag on any corner or side *handle*—the small boxes on the corners and sides of the image. This resizes the *image* but does not change the size of the image *file.* If you want to *resave* the image file, click the Resample button in the Picture toolbar (identified and explained in Step 14 of this chapter).

Step 12: Locate and Align Pictures

Very often, you'll want to flow text around a picture. You can do this by aligning pictures on the left or right side of your page. When you *right-align* a picture, text flows around it to the left, and vice versa. Figure 5-10 shows a right-aligned image in FrontPage.

Follow the steps listed next to align a picture.

Figure 5-10
A right-aligned picture, with text flowing around the left

Custom Work ¶

▣Steve Belsito specializes in handcrafted mission-style reproduction household furniture. Specializing in Morris Chairs, dining room sets, coffee tables and bookcases. The San Francisco Chronicle wrote: "... **Belsito's reproductions are so**

1. Select a picture in Page view.

2. Click the Align Left or Align Right icons in the Formatting toolbar to assign either left- or right-alignment to the picture.

3. After you align a picture, you can still move it around on a page by clicking and dragging the picture.

Locating Aligned Image Insertion Points

The small right and left arrow icons at the beginning of paragraphs mark the location of picture files, and they indicate that they are right- and left-aligned.

Step 13: Create Thumbnails

Thumbnails are small versions of a larger picture. Since pictures take time to download, you can make your pages download faster by displaying small thumbnails instead of full pictures on your pages. Visitors wanting to see a full-sized image just click on the thumbnail, which serves as a link.

FrontPage comes with a handy feature that automatically converts an image into a thumbnail, and automatically generates a link to the full-sized version of the image.

To convert a picture into a thumbnail, follow these steps:

1. Select Tools | Page Options and click on the AutoThumbnail tab.

2. From the Set drop-down list, choose the dimension that you want FrontPage to use when resizing your thumbnail (Width, Height, Shortest Side, or Longest Side).

3. In the Pixels box, enter the size that you want your thumbnail reduced to, as shown in Figure 5-11.

Figure 5-II
Defining
thumbnail size

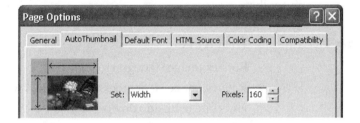

4   If you wish, you can also define a border or assign a beveling effect for your thumbnail, using checkboxes in the AutoThumbnail tab.

5. After you define the size (and optional features) of your thumbnail, click OK to close the dialog box.

6. Select a picture.

7. Choose Tools | Auto Thumbnail. Your image is automatically reduced to the size you defined for thumbnails.

Step 14: Edit Pictures in FrontPage

In addition to defining picture properties, you can edit the appearance of an image right in FrontPage. The picture editing tools are limited but useful for things like flipping an image, sharpening up contrast, or cropping a picture.

The tools for editing pictures are on the Picture toolbar. When you select an image, the Picture toolbar appears (if the Picture toolbar isn't visible with a picture selected, choose View | Toolbars | Pictures to display it). The Picture toolbar includes tools you can use to edit your image, and is illustrated in Figure 5-12, along with a few of the picture editing tools.

Figure 5-12
Some of the editing
tools available on
the Picture toolbar

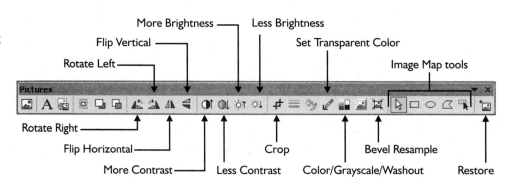

The following table briefly explains the most useful picture editing tools on the toolbar:

Picture Toolbar Tool	What It Does
Rotate Right	Rotates image 90 degrees clockwise
Rotate Left	Rotates image 90 degrees counter-clockwise
Flip Horizontal	Flips image upside down
Flip Vertical	Flips image right to left
More Contrast	Sharpens contrast; brights get brighter, darks get darker
Less Contrast	Reduces contrast, bright and dark colors are muted
Crop	Place a cropping marquee over the image. Resize the crop marquee by dragging on handles, then click the Crop tool again to cut away everything outside the crop marquee.
Set Transparent Color	Use the wand that appears to click on one color in an image to make that color disappear (so the page background shows through). JPEGs will be converted to GIFs if you use the Transparent tool.
Color	Toggles between displaying original color (automatic), or black and white, grayscale, or washout (faded)
Bevel	Produces a 3-D effect on the edges of the picture
Resample	Changes the original file—see warning described next!
Image Map tools	Enables you to draw clickable hotspots on an image that serve as links and are defined like other links
Restore	Restores the image to the saved file

Warning! Resampling Permanently Changes Your Image

If you make a picture smaller in FrontPage, you can reduce the file size of that picture by clicking the Resample button in the Picture toolbar. This speeds up your page download time. However, resampling can overwrite your original image file when you save your web page. So, if you resample a picture, it's best to make sure you have a copy of the original image saved somewhere outside your FrontPage web folder.

Step 15: Setting Picture Properties

You can define important image attributes in the Picture Properties dialog box. Alternative representation text (Alt text) is the text that appears as a ToolTip when a visitor hovers over a picture or when a picture is viewed in a web page reader or browser that does not support pictures.

Horizontal and vertical spacing creates space between a left- or right-aligned picture and the text that flows around it. Border size defines how thick a border (if any) appears around your picture.

Other image attributes control how the file is managed when it loads into a browser. Interlacing "fades in" GIF images instead of having them download line by line. Setting Progressive Passes creates a similar effect for JPEG images.

To access the Picture Properties dialog box for a selected image, choose Format | Properties from the menu bar.

Don't Use the Picture Properties Dialog Box for Movies

There are three tabs in the Image Properties dialog box: General, Video, and Appearance. As explained later in this chapter in the section "Embed Media in Your Page," you should avoid the Insert | Picture | Video menu option when embedding video into your pages. Therefore, the Video tab of the Pictures Properties dialog box is not really useful.

As explained earlier, you can assign left or right alignment to a picture simply by using the Align Left and Align Right buttons in the Formatting toolbar. Use the None icon in the Appearance tab to remove alignment. Use the Specify Size checkbox in the Appearance tab to activate the Width and Height boxes and set the size of your selected picture by entering either pixels or percentage sizes.

The Appearance tab also lets you define border thickness and spacing around a picture. A good place to start is by assigning five pixels of horizontal spacing and three pixels of vertical spacing around a picture. Figure 5-13 shows horizontal and vertical spacing being set.

Figure 5-13
Defining image
spacing

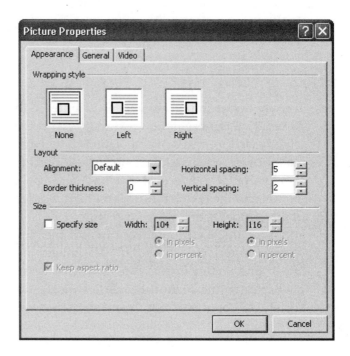

Finally, you can define picture border thickness in the Appearance tab of the Picture Properties dialog box by entering a value in the Border Thickness box. To remove a border, enter **0** (zero).

Use the General tab of the Picture Properties dialog box to define image type, alternative representation text, or links. Use the GIF or JPEG radio buttons to change the file format of a selected image. To define alternative representation text (often referred to as Alt text), enter text in the Text box in the Alternative Representations section of the General tab, as shown in Figure 5-14.

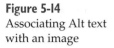

Figure 5-14
Associating Alt text
with an image

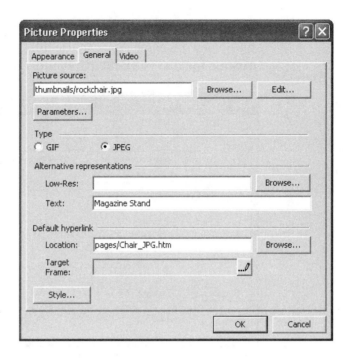

Other picture formatting options in the General tab let you define a low-resolution alternative representation for your picture—a smaller file size version of your picture.

It's easier to define links for a picture in the Define Hyperlink dialog box than it is in the Picture Properties dialog box—refer to the section "Define Text and Picture Links" in this chapter to associate a link with a picture.

Step 16: Save Pictures in FrontPage

If you copy and paste an image into FrontPage, that image will be saved as a GIF or JPEG when you save your web page. In addition, if you edited and resampled an image in FrontPage, that image file will be saved *with the new attributes you changed when you edited the image.* You *do* have the option of renaming an edited image when you save it, and leaving the original image file unchanged in your web folder. These steps explain how to save images on your page.

I. Choose File | Save. The Save Embedded Files dialog box appears with a list of images on your page that need to be saved.

2. If you want to save an image with a new filename, click Rename and type a new filename. You can use this feature to avoid overwriting an existing file that you edited in FrontPage, as shown in Figure 5-15.

Figure 5-15
Renaming an
image file

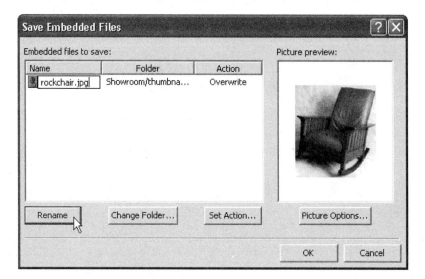

3. Click the Change Folder button to save your image to a different folder in your web. This button opens the Change Folder dialog box, where you can select a folder.

4. Click the Set Action button and select the Use Existing radio button in the Set Action dialog box to revert to the previously saved version of your picture.

5. Click the Picture Options button to change the file format and file format settings to for the picture in the Picture Options dialog box.

6. When you have examined and—if necessary changed—your picture file settings, click OK to close the Save Embedded Files dialog box and save pictures embedded in your web page.

TIPS OF THE TRADE

Setting Picture Options in FrontPage

The Picture Options dialog box allows you to change an image to GIF or JPEG format, and to define image settings like GIF transparency and inter-lacing, or JPEG quality or progressive passes. Refer to Chapter 3 for a brief explanation of these options.

Step 17: Define Text and Picture Links

The backbone of a good web site is a logical, easy-to-follow set of links that help a visitor navigate to and from pages in your site. In Chapter 1, you learned the basic principles of planning a link structure for your site. In addition, links to resources on web pages outside your site can add value to your site.

FrontPage makes it very simple to create links to pages outside your site. Anything you type on a page that starts with www and ends with .com, .org, .net, or another web site file extension will automatically be converted to a link. This is true for e-mail addresses as well. When you type anything that looks like an e-mail address, FrontPage will convert it to a link.

Often, of course, you'll want to link text other than a URL. To do that, first select the text that will serve as the link, and then click the Insert Hyperlink button on the toolbar.

Links? Hyperlinks?

FrontPage uses the term *hyperlink* in place of the more commonly used and simpler term *link*. They're the same thing.

The Insert Hyperlink dialog box opens when you click the Insert Hyperlink button. Enter a web site address (or e-mail address) in the Address box to define a link to a URL.

To define a link to a page (or file) in your own web site, follow these steps:

1. Select text or a picture.

2. Click the Insert Hyperlink button in the Standard toolbar.

3. Click on Existing File Or Web Page in the Link To column of the dialog box.

4. Choose the Current Folder box in the Look In area.

5. Navigate to the page you want to link to in the list of files displayed in the dialog box, as shown in Figure 5-16.

Figure 5-16
Defining a link

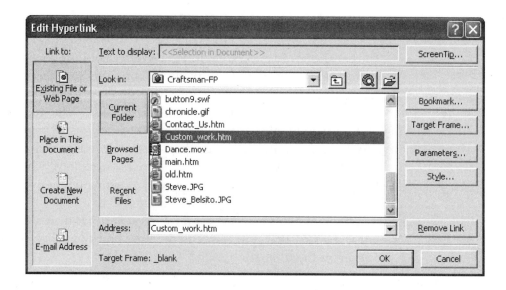

6. With your link selected, click OK or stay in the dialog box to define a target window and a screen tip for your link.

7. By default, links open in the same browser window as the linked text. To open a link in a *new* browser window, click the Target Frame button and select New Window in the Target Frame dialog box, as shown in Figure 5-17. Then click OK to close the Target Link dialog box.

Figure 5-17
Setting a link to open in a new browser window

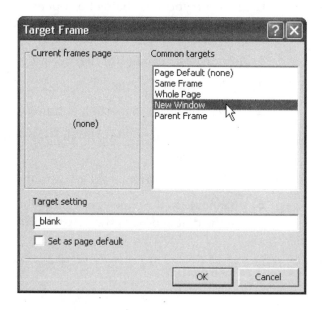

8. To define pop-up text that displays when a visitor hovers over your link, click the ScreenTip button in the Insert Hyperlink dialog box, and type text in the Set Hyperlink ScreenTip. Then click OK to return to the Insert Hyperlink dialog box. ScreenTips look like the text in Figure 5-18.

Figure 5-18
A ScreenTip displays when link text is scrolled over.

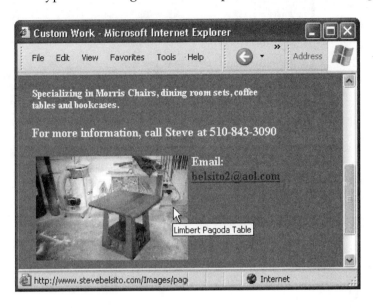

Screen Tips vs. Alt Text

If you assign Alt text to a picture, you cannot also assign a visible ScreenTip—when the image is scrolled over, the Alt text will appear, not the ScreenTip.

9. Click OK to finish defining your link.

Step 18: Create Image Maps

Image maps have many clickable areas that are defined using the Rectangular Hotspot, Circular Hotspot, or Polygonal Hotspot tools in the Picture toolbar. Follow the steps listed here to create an image map:

1. Select a picture. If the picture toolbar isn't visible, choose View | Toolbars | Pictures.

2. In the Picture toolbar, click the Rectangular Hotspot button.

3. Click and drag on your picture to draw a rectangle around an area that will be a hotspot, as shown in Figure 5-19.

Figure 5-19
Drawing a
rectangular image
map hotspot

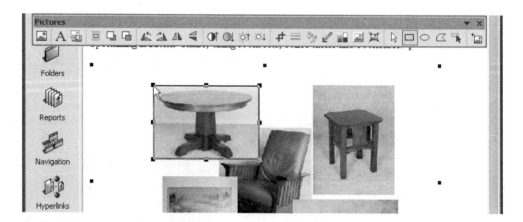

4. When you release your mouse button, the Insert Hyperlink dialog box appears. Navigate to a web page to link the hotspot to, or enter an external URL (web site) in the Address area of the dialog box, and then click OK.

5. After you finish the image map, test your links in the Preview tab of Page view.

TIPS OF THE TRADE

Oval or Odd Shaped Hotspots

You can add a circular hotspot by using the Circular Hotspot tool, or you can add an irregularly shaped hotspot by using the Polygonal Hotspot tool. To use the Polygonal tool, click several times to outline the hotspot, and double-click when you've completed the outline.

Step 19: Embed Media in Your Page

Audio files—and especially video files—can be *very* large. So, before including them in your web site, you'll need to be certain that your web server has room for them. Refer to the discussion of video in the section "Shopping for a Web Host" in Chapter 2 to make sure your web host can handle your video files. For a discussion of how to get audio and video files for the web, refer to the sections "Preparing Sound Files for Your Web Site" and "Preparing Video for the Web," both in Chapter 3.

If you've got audio and video files in your FrontPage web folder, and your server is ready for these files, the easiest way to present your media files is to simply create a link to those files. That link will open the files in a new browser window. Follow these steps to create a link to a media file:

1. With your web page open, select text or a picture to link to the media file.

2. Click the Insert Hyperlink button to open the Insert Hyperlink dialog box.

3. In the Insert Hyperlink dialog box, navigate to the folder with your video file.

4. Select a video file and click OK to close the Insert Hyperlink dialog box.

5. Save your page and test the link in a web browser. Your movie or sound file will play using whatever plug-in media software is configured for your system.

That's the easy way to include media files in your site. For a more sophisticated and integrated use of media, you can embed a media plug-in right on your page and display a video (or the controls of a sound player) in your page. Figure 5-20 has both a sound file player and a video player embedded in a page.

Figure 5-20
Embedded media in a page

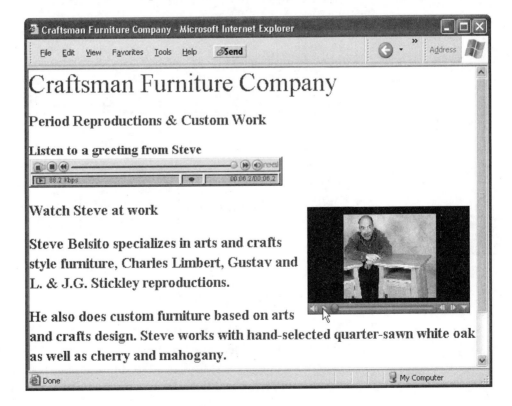

Follow these steps to embed a video in an open page.

1. Place your insertion point where you want the video to appear in your page.

2. Choose Insert | Web Component and click Advanced Controls.

3. From the Choose a Control section of the Insert Web Component dialog box, select Plug-In.

4. Click the Finish button to open the Plug-In Properties dialog box.

5. Use the Browse button in the Plug-In Properties dialog box to select a media file to embed, as shown in Figure 5-21.

Figure 5-21
Selecting a video
to embed in a page

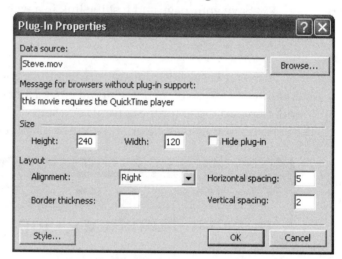

6. In the Message for Browsers Without Plug-In Support area, type a message to display for visitors whose browsers do not support your video format.

7. Enter a size for the plug-in display in the Height and Width areas.

Don't Hide Your Video
Don't select the Hide Plug-In checkbox. If you do, FrontPage will hide your media in browsers.

8. You can align videos the same way you align pictures. Left-aligned movies will have text flow around them on the right, and right-aligned videos will have text flow around them on the left. Use the Alignment drop-down menu to select Left or Right.

9. If you want to display a visible border around your image, enter a value (in pixels) in the Border Thickness area.

10. You can define a buffer between your media plug-in and text that is adjacent to the plug-in by entering values (in pixels) in the Horizontal Spacing and Vertical Spacing areas.

11. When you have finished defining plug-in properties, click OK to embed the plug-in on your page. Your plug-in will display as an icon. Preview your media file in the Preview tab of Page view.

You can edit plug-in properties by selecting a plug-in icon in Normal Page view and choosing Format | Properties.

Step 20: Use Tables for Page Layout

Tables are the most reliable way to position objects on a web page. Some of the most common design techniques include laying text out in table columns, positioning an image at an exact spot by placing it in a table cell, and constraining the width of your web page by enclosing the entire page content in a table.

Tables used for page layout usually have the table border, as well as cell borders, concealed. The table acts as an *invisible* structure organizing where objects are positioned on a page.

Table properties are defined on two basic levels in FrontPage—you can define properties for the *entire table* like background color, cell padding, and cell spacing. And you can define properties for a *specific cell* (or group of cells). Cell properties include horizontal and vertical alignment, background color (which can be different than that of the table background), and height and width.

**TIPS OF
THE TRADE**

Start with a Table

Most professional web designers start by constraining the *entire content* of a page in a table. That way, you can control the width of your page *regardless of what size monitor is used to view your site*. For example, if you want to display your page content in an 800-pixel-wide monitor, you could constrain your page width to 780 pixels by placing the content in a 780-pixel-wide table (the extra 20 pixels allows for onscreen elements like scrollbars). After you constrain your page content in a table, you can locate objects on your page by placing other tables within that table.

Follow these steps to create a table to define page size, and then to include a table within the table to position objects.

1. Define a table to constrain your page content by placing your cursor at the top of your page and choosing Table | Insert | Table. The Insert Table dialog box appears.

2. Enter **1** in the Rows and **1** in the Columns boxes.

3. Check the Specify Width checkbox and enter table width in the box below, as shown in Figure 5-22. Enter a page width (like 780 pixels). Table height will expand to fit the content placed in the table.

Figure 5-22
Defining a one-cell table to control page width

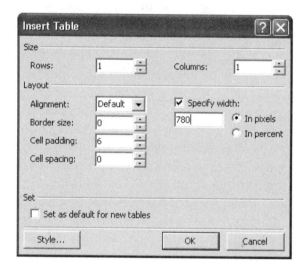

TIPS OF THE TRADE

Pixels? Or Percent?

Table width can be defined in pixels or percent. Pixels provide absolute control of table width—780 pixels will be the same width on a monitor that displays 1600 pixels in width, or one that displays 1040 pixels in width. Tables with width defined as percent change size depending on the size of the window in which they are viewed—so a 50% table would be 800 pixels wide in a maximized browser window on a 1600-pixel computer, but only 520 pixels wide in a maximized browser window on a 1040-pixel-wide monitor.

4.   Normally, no border is visible when tables are used to control page size or the location of objects. So, select **0** in the Border Size box.

5.   Cell padding defines space between the cell content and the edge of a cell. It's useful for keeping content from bumping into other content in your table. Start by defining cell spacing at 6 pixels; you can adjust this later if you wish.

6.   Cell spacing creates space between cells in a table. Normally, cell spacing is not used when tables are created for page design, so enter **0** in the Cell Spacing box. Then click OK to generate your table.

7.   Edit table properties by right-clicking on your table and choosing Table Properties from the context menu. You can redefine table size and other attributes in the Table Properties dialog box. You can also assign a background color from the Background Color drop-down palette, as shown in Figure 5-23.

Figure 5-23
Defining a table
background color

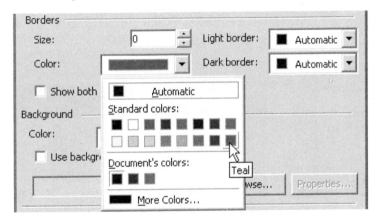

Step 21: Use Table Cells to Place Objects on a Page

The grid created by rows and columns of cells in a table can be used to place blocks of text, images, or even media at a set point on a page. For example, if you wanted to place a block of text in the middle of a page, you could create a three-row, three-column table, and place the content in the middle cell of the second row.

1.   To create a multicell table, choose Table | Insert | Table, and define numbers of rows and columns in the Rows and Columns boxes. Click OK to generate the table.

2. Resize cell height or width by clicking and dragging on the lines between cells (these lines are visible in FrontPage Page view but won't be visible in a browser if you selected 0 border size and 0 cell spacing).

3. Change cell properties by right-clicking in a cell (or group of selected cells) and choosing Cell Properties from the context menu. The default vertical formatting for cells is centered. To align cell content at the top of a cell, set the Vertical alignment box to Top. (To center, left- , or right-align cell content, just use the alignment buttons in the Formatting toolbar).

4. Set cell background colors with the Background Color drop-down palette.

5. After you define cell properties for a selected cell (or group of cells), click OK in the Cell Properties dialog box.

Figure 5-24 shows a page laid out with one large table enclosing a three-column table to display text and pictures, and a one-row, five-column table on the bottom used as a navigation bar.

Figure 5-24
Different cell background colors help break up the page.

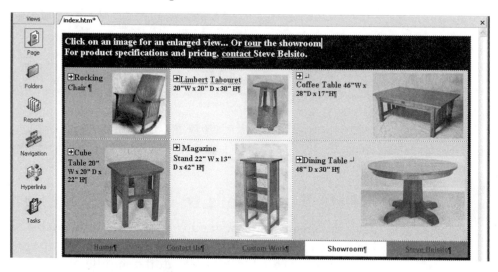

Step 22: Publish Your Web

Once you have created your FrontPage web on your local computer, you can publish all or part of that content to your remote web site. To review the process of obtaining web server space, see the section "Buying Server Space" in Chapter 2. Before you upload to your server, make sure you know the following information from your web host provider:

1. What is your URL?

2. What is your username?

3. What is your password?

If you have that information, you're ready to publish your web content using the following steps:

1. Choose File | Publish Web. If you have not yet logged in to your web site, the Publish Destination dialog box will appear (if you are already logged on to your site, skip ahead to the next step). Enter the URL for your site (*including http://*) in the Enter Publish Destination area of the dialog box and click OK. FrontPage will connect with the URL you entered. The Connect To dialog box appears. Enter your user name and password in the Connect To dialog box, as shown in Figure 5-25.

Figure 5-25
Logging in to
a FrontPage
remote web site

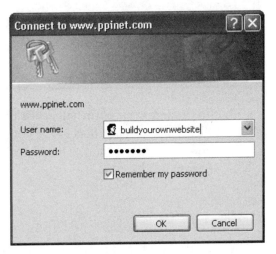

If FrontPage Doesn't Find FrontPage Extensions at Your Server

If FrontPage doesn't find FrontPage extensions at your server, you'll see an error message informing you that your server "does not appear to have FrontPage server extensions installed." If that happens, contact your web server and ask them to correct the problem by installing FrontPage extensions for your site.

2. Once you have successfully logged in to your site, you can publish your content to the remote server. The Publish Web dialog box appears in a separate window and displays the content of your local site (on the left) and your remote site (on the right), as shown in Figure 5-26.

Figure 5-26
Local and remote site content are displayed in the Publish Web dialog box.

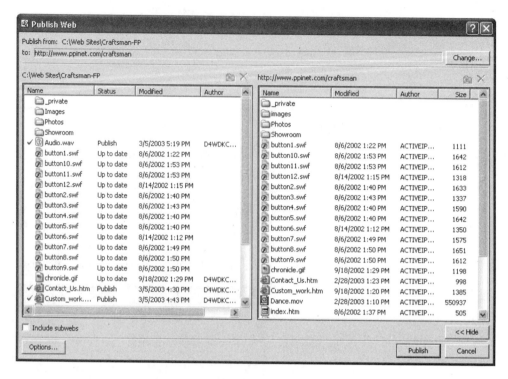

3. To publish your entire site, click the Publish button. To publish selected files, click to select files in the left side of the Publish Web dialog box, and drag them from the left (local) side of the dialog box to the right (remote) side.

TIPS OF THE TRADE

Changing Upload Options

By default, FrontPage only publishes (uploads) changed pages, and uses local pages to replace remote pages. You can change those options by clicking on the Options button in the Publish Web dialog box, and selecting other upload defaults in the General tab of the Options dialog box. After you do so, click OK to return to the Publish Web dialog box.

TESTING 1-2-3

To build web sites in FrontPage, you need to have FrontPage installed on your computer. You also need to have FrontPage extensions installed on your server. This is a service provided by your web hosting company, who will provide you with a FrontPage user name and password to log in to your site.

Chapter 6

Creating Web Pages Using Dreamweaver

Tools of the Trade

Before you can create a web site with Dreamweaver, your site must support File Transfer Protocol (FTP) and you must have installed Dreamweaver software for PC or Macintosh. The optimal environment for developing web sites with Dreamweaver is to use Dreamweaver MX with Windows MX. (The Windows version of Dreamweaver MX incorporates some helpful interface features such as tabbed pages so you can more easily work on many pages at once.) However, the steps in this chapter will work just fine (with some minor modifications) with Dreamweaver 3, 4, or MX running on either Mac or PC. In addition, you'll need an Internet connection to upload your site to your web server.

Even before you launch Dreamweaver, you should organize all the files that will be included in your web site into a single folder (which can also contain subfolders) on your computer. Dreamweaver needs to know which folder is the *home* folder for your site—the main folder. Dreamweaver refers to this folder as your *local site*.

After you have organized your files into a folder, launch Dreamweaver.

Step 1: Defining a Dreamweaver Site

The Dreamweaver interface is overwhelming, even to experienced users. Many features—including features rarely used—are accessed by *panels* that by default are docked on the right side of the Dreamweaver window. Before you start work, you can reduce some of the chaos and confusion by choosing Window | Hide Panels.

After that bit of optional housekeeping, you're ready to define your site. Choose Site | New Site. The Site Definition dialog box appears.

The Site Definition dialog box in Dreamweaver MX includes two tabs: Basic and Advanced. If you are setting up a basic web site (as opposed to a complex site that incorporates content from an online database), it's easiest to bypass the wizard process and simply define your Dreamweaver *site* (your local home folder) by clicking the Advanced tab, shown in Figure 6-1.

Figure 6-1
Defining a web site using the Advanced tab

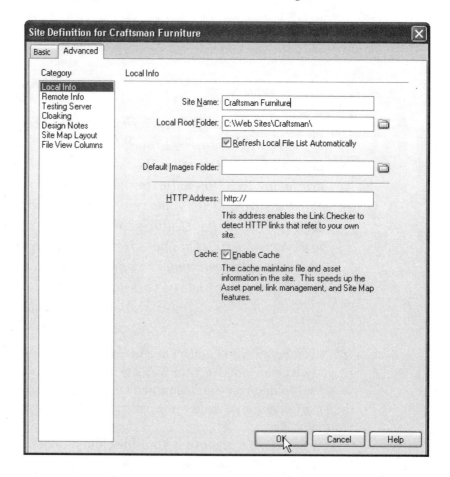

In the Site Name area of the dialog box, type a name for your site. This can be anything that helps you identify the site. Then click the Folder icon next to the Local Root Folder area to navigate to the folder containing your files.

Selecting the Refresh Local File List Automatically checkbox synchronizes the files on your local computer with the display of files in Dreamweaver. Select this checkbox, and then click OK to close the dialog box.

Now that you've defined the Local Info section of your web site in the Site Definition dialog, you're ready to start creating a web page.

The Site panel in Dreamweaver, shown in Figure 6-2, shows all the files in your web site. In Dreamweaver MX, the Site panel displays on the right side of the Dreamweaver window. You can collapse the Site panel by clicking the right arrow on the left side of the Site panel. You can expand the Site panel to fill your Dreamweaver window by clicking the Expand/Collapse button in the icon bar on top of the Site panel.

Figure 6-2
Expanding
the Site panel

Click here to expand or collapse the Site panel

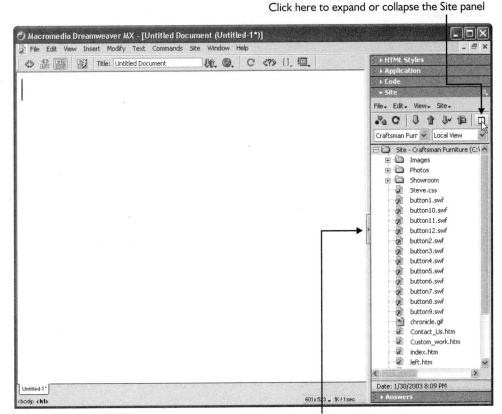

Click here to hide or view the Site panel

You can collapse the expanded Site panel by clicking the Expand/Collapse icon again in the Site panel.

Step 2: Formatting Text in Dreamweaver

You can create a new web page by choosing File, New (if you have expanded the Site panel, collapse it before creating a new file). Accept all the defaults to create a new web page from scratch. After you create a web page, you can open it from the Site panel by double-clicking it.

As you type and edit pages, you'll want to save your work. To do that, choose File | Save. The first time you save a page file, you'll be prompted to type in a filename. Make sure the filename includes an *.htm* or *.html* extension, so that Dreamweaver (and web browsers) will know that this file is coded in HTML.

You can copy and paste text into Dreamweaver, or you can enter and edit the text right in Dreamweaver itself.

TIPS OF THE TRADE

Importing Word Files into Dreamweaver

Dreamweaver offers the option of importing text from a Microsoft Word document that has been saved as HTML. In general, you'll find it much simpler to copy and paste text from Word into Dreamweaver, as shown next. When you copy and paste text into Dreamweaver, some minimal text formatting attributes—such as paragraph and line breaks—are maintained when the text is pasted into Dreamweaver.

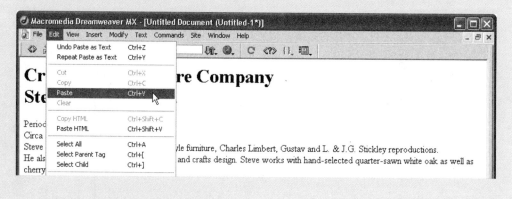

If you choose to create text in Dreamweaver, simply type it into the open page.

TIPS OF THE TRADE

Fixing Paragraph Breaks

Sometimes when you paste text into Dreamweaver, paragraph breaks are corrupted. You can insert a paragraph break, as you would in any word processing program, by placing your cursor in text and pressing ENTER. You can also remove a line or paragraph break by using the DELETE key.

After you've entered text, you can assign fonts, font size, font color, and paragraph attributes by selecting the text and using Dreamweaver's Properties inspector. The Properties inspector is the single most useful element of the Dreamweaver interface. To view the Properties inspector (if it's not visible), choose Window | Properties.

TIPS OF THE TRADE

Choosing a Font

A limited set of fonts are available in Dreamweaver because web designers are constrained by the "browser-safe" fonts that they know will be available on most visitors computers. This set of fonts includes some form of Times/Times Roman, some form of Arial/Helvetica, and some form of Courier.

In Dreamweaver, fonts are grouped in sets of three; each font in a set can be used as an alternative to another font in the same set if a visitor to your site does not have the primary assigned font installed on his or her system:

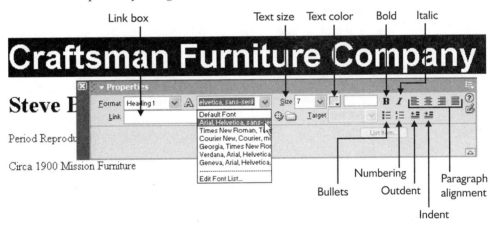

You can select from among seven font sizes from the Properties inspector, as shown next. Theses fonts sizes are not listed in point size, as you might expect, but in general size increments: size 2 displays as 10-point text, size 3 displays as 12-point text, and larger sizes display as larger fonts. These point equivalents, however, depend on the settings in a visitor's web browser. The relative, visitor-defined nature of font sizes makes it difficult for web designers to control exactly how a page will look, but relative font sizes make content much more accessible to vision-impaired visitors who have adjusted fonts to appear larger on their screens. In short, you cannot define the *exact* size of a font using the Properties inspector, but you can define a size that works within your design and that will appear the same size relative to the rest of the text and design in a viewer's browser.

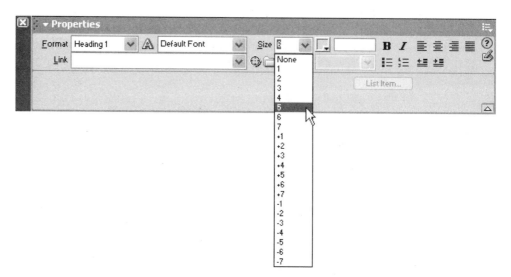

To assign colors to selected text, click the Text Color swatch in the Properties inspector, as shown next. A palette opens, displaying 216 *browser-safe colors* that are supported by most operating systems and browser environments.

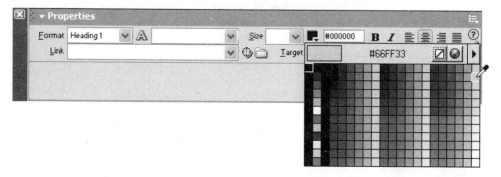

In normal web page formatting, one line is inserted between each paragraph. You can change this by using a line break instead of a paragraph break at the end of a line. To do this, simply hold down the SHIFT key while you press the ENTER key. The drawback to using line breaks instead of paragraph breaks is that any paragraph formatting you apply to a section of text separated by line breaks (such as centering, for instance) will apply to the *entire* paragraph, even those sections that are separated by line breaks.

To align text left, center, right, or fully justified, click inside a paragraph, and then click one of the paragraph alignment buttons in the Properties inspector:

To indent a paragraph, click the Text Indent button in the Properties panel. To undo indenting, click the Text Outdent button.

The Bullets button in the Properties inspector, shown in Figure 6-3, assigns bullets to the left of selected paragraphs. The Numbering button next to it assigns sequential numbers. These tools also indent paragraphs and assign single-spacing to them.

Figure 6-3
Creating a
bulleted list

Step 3: Embedding Images and Media in Web Pages

You can insert an image onto a page by choosing Insert | Image and navigating to the image in the Select Image Source dialog box. In this dialog box, select the

File System radio button in the Select File Name From area. Then, in the Look In drop-down menu, navigate to a folder on your local computer and select an image to place on the page. Click the Preview Images checkbox to display a preview of the selected image, along with the size of the image in pixels, the file size, and download time, which is calculated based on the download speed default setting of 28.8 kilobits per second (Kbps).

TIPS OF THE TRADE

Changing Connection Speed Changes Download Time

You can change the download connection speed used to calculate download times by choosing Edit | Preferences in Windows or Mac OS 9, or by choosing Edit | Dreamweaver MX Preferences in Mac OSX. Choose Status Bar in the Category list of the Preferences dialog box, and then choose a different modem speed in the Connection Speed drop-down list.

After you have selected an image to embed on your page, select the document from the Relative To drop-down list in the Select Image Source dialog box to enable Dreamweaver to adjust the linkage between your image and your page—this is especially handy if you've renamed either of them in the Site panel. (See Figure 6-4.) When everything is set, click OK in the Select Image Source dialog box to place the image on your page.

Figure 6-4
Placing an image on your page

Troubleshooting Busted Image Links

If the connection between an embedded image and a page has been corrupted, Dreamweaver (and web browsers) will display an X in the space where the image should go. No need to panic, though, because this linkage can be broken for a variety of reasons. If this happens, you can simply reinsert the image on your page and resave the page.

After you have placed an image on the page, you can select that image to display the Properties inspector with formatting features available for images. An image name is not generally necessary—unless you are incorporating your image into a JavaScript. On the other hand, it doesn't hurt to assign a name—just make sure that you avoid using spaces and special characters. Mac and PCs file names can include spaces and special characters, but many web servers use versions of the Unix/Linux operating system that will not recognize file names with spaces or special characters.

It's best to edit your image size in a file *before* you bring it into Dreamweaver. Enlarging images in Dreamweaver can make them grainy and blurry because the image file only represents a set number of pixels (tiny dots). Enlarging an image creates more space between these pixels, resulting in a blurry image. Reducing the size of an image in Dreamweaver does not reduce image quality, but it doesn't save file size either, because the image file retains all the information needed for the original image size. But if you need to change an image size after you've placed the image in a Dreamweaver page, you can select the image and click and drag a corner or side handles, as shown in Figure 6-5. (Use a corner handle for resizing, and hold down the SHIFT key as you resize to maintain your original height-to-width ratio.)

Figure 6-5
Resizing an image

You can move an image on the page by clicking and dragging. However, you'll find that, by default, images do not allow text to flow around them. Instead, text will appear above and below the image.

You can make text flow around an image by aligning the image left or right. (Technically, other alignment options are available for images, but they don't have much practical use in page design.) Figure 6-6 shows a right-aligned image with text aligned left. With an image selected, choose Left or Right from the Align drop-down list in the Properties inspector to make the text flow around the image. When you align a picture, an icon appears on the page at the point where the image *is inserted* (not where it appears on the page if text flows around it). Click and drag that icon to move an aligned image to a different part of the page, while maintaining text flow around the image.

Figure 6-6
Flowing text to the left of an image by aligning the image to the right

Images generally look better if you separate them from adjacent text with height and width spacing. You can add spacing on the sides and/or top and bottom of an image by typing values in the H Space (horizontal spacing) or V Space (vertical spacing) boxes in the Properties inspector, shown next.

Space Your Images

Typically, web designers will assign 5 pixels of horizontal spacing and 3 pixels of vertical spacing to separate an image from surrounding text. But feel free to experiment.

Image borders are defined by the value in the Border area of the Properties inspector for a selected image. By default, border coloring is defined by the color you assign to the text adjacent to your image.

The Alt area in the Properties inspector allows you to create text that can be read out loud using special software. This is helpful for visitors to your site who are sight-impaired. Alt text also displays in Internet Explorer if a visitor rolls the mouse over the image. In addition, Alt text displays while a large image downloads, or if for some reason an image link is broken and the picture cannot display at all.

To assign Alt text to your image, type in text in the Alt box in the Properties inspector for a selected image:

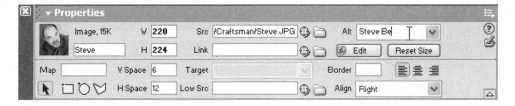

The Alt text won't be visible in Dreamweaver, but you can see it if you preview your page in Internet Explorer or another web browser. Dreamweaver provides a close approximation of how your page will look. But as your page formatting grows more complex, you'll want to rely on previewing your page in a browser to see exactly how it will look to visitors.

To preview a page in one of your installed web browsers, choose File | Preview in Browser, and select a browser. Your image may look similar to the one shown in Figure 6-7.

Figure 6-7
Previewing your
page in Internet
Explorer—and
testing Alt text

Small images that have been designed to *tile* (repeat across the page) can be
used as page backgrounds. You can tile an image as a page background in an
open page by choosing Modify | Page Properties to open the Page Properties
dialog box. Click the Browse button next to the Background Image box to navigate to an image file. Click OK to select the image, as shown in Figure 6-8, and
click OK again to close the dialog box. Your selected background image will now
be tiled across the page.

Figure 6-8
Assigning a tiling
background image
to a page

Embedding video or animation in a web page is similar to placing an image. These embedded movies appear in a web page along with player controls. In the section "Preparing Video for the Web" in Chapter 3, you learned that videos play in whatever video *plug-in*—media player—your visitor has configured to play audio or video on his or her operating system.

To embed a movie in a web page, click in the page where you want the movie to appear and choose Insert | Media | Plug-In from the pop-up menu. In the Select File dialog box, shown in Figure 6-9, navigate to a video file. Select the file or type its name into the File Name box, and then click OK to close the dialog.

Figure 6-9
Selecting a video
file to embed in
a web page

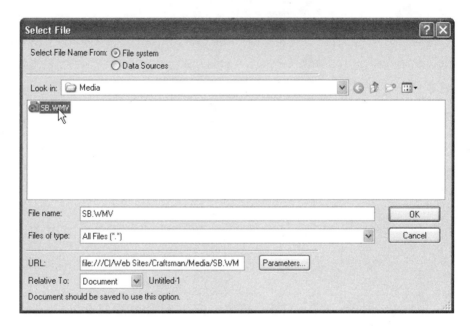

If the movie is outside of your local site folder, you'll be prompted to copy the file to your local site folder. When the dialog box prompting you to save the file to your site folder appears, click Yes, and then navigate to a folder within your site. Click Save in the Copy File dialog box to save the file to your site.

You can resize the embedded movie by selecting the plug-in icon and holding down the SHIFT key while clicking and dragging on a side or corner handle. Preview the movie by clicking the Play button in the Properties inspector for a selected movie. You can add information to the W and H boxes in the Properties inspector to define the width and height, respectively, of the movie in pixels. The Src area locates the video file. The Plg URL box is used to define a URL (web address) to display if a visitor needs to download a plug-in player to see the movie. Figure 6-10 shows a movie being previewed in Dreamweaver. When the movie is playing, the Play button becomes a Stop button.

Figure 6-10
The Play button
in the Properties
inspector is available
when a plug-in
movie is selected.

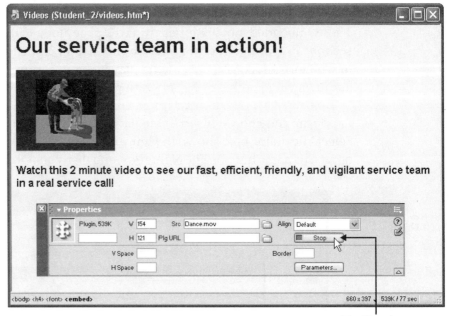

Play/Stop button

You can align movies so that text flows around them as you align images—simply use the Align drop-down list in the Properties inspector to align a video left or right. The V (vertical) and H (horizontal) Space boxes can be used to create space between the video and surrounding text. Use the Border box in the Properties inspector to define border thickness in pixels.

Step 4: Creating Links for Images and Text

Text or images can be used to define links that can be clicked to open other web pages, images, media, or other files in a web browser.

To assign a link to text, first select the text. You can enter a URL in the Link box in the Properties inspector if the link is to a page or file outside of your site. To link to a file in your web site, click the Browse for File icon to the right of the Link area (the icon that looks like a folder). Then, in the Select File dialog box, locate and select the file to which you are linking the selected text, as shown in Figure 6-11. After you've selected a file to which you want to link the text, click OK to define the link.

Figure 6-11
Defining a text
link to a page in
your web site

To link an image, you can define a link in the Properties inspector for the selected image the same way you defined a link for selected text.

Normally, linked pages open in the same browser window as the page with the original link. You can, however, define links that open in a new browser window. This has the advantage of keeping your original page open in a visitor's computer while he or she follows your link. The disadvantage is that links that open in a new browser window do not have an active Back button. To go back, the visitor must return to the main browser window.

To set a link to open in a new browser window, in the Properties inspector, choose _blank from the Target drop-down list for the link:

Step 5: Formatting Page Properties

Page properties can be used to format your page background color, margins, page title, default font color, and text link colors. To access the Page Properties dialog box that controls all these features, choose Modify | Page Properties.

To set a page background color, click the Background color swatch and select a color from the palette of browser-safe colors. To set a default text color for your page, click the Text color swatch and choose a color from the palette. You can define custom colors for the Links, Visited Links (those that a visitor has already visited), and Active Links (whereby color displays when a link is being clicked) using the color swatches in the Page Properties dialog box as well, as shown in Figure 6-12.

Figure 6-12
Defining a page background color, default page text color, and customized colors for link text

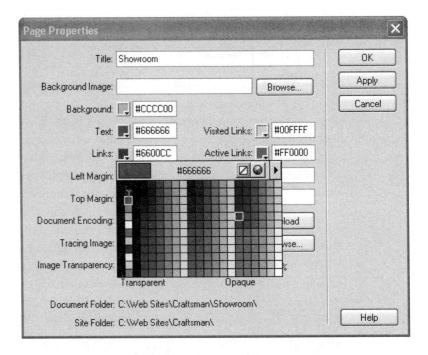

Normally, a 10-pixel margin appears along the top and left margins of the page. If you want your pages content to fill the entire browser window with no margin, you can change the margin to zero. In the Page Properties dialog box (choose Modify | Page Settings if it's not already open), enter values of **0** (zero) in the Left Margin, Top Margin, Margin Width, and Margin Height areas. When you do this, Dreamweaver generates HTML coding for both Netscape and Internet Explorer browsers.

Page titles are an important element of every web page, and you define them in the Page Properties dialog box as well. Titles are the text that appears in the title bar of a visitor's browser window. Page titles can include quotes, commas, spaces, or any other characters.

Keywords are text that is used by search engines to find and list your site. Descriptions are used by search engines to describe your page in a search results list. Define keywords for an open page by choosing Insert | Head Tags | Keywords. Enter keywords, separated by commas, in the Keywords dialog box:

To define a page description for search engines, choose Insert | Head Tags | Description. Enter a normal paragraph to describe your page in the Page Description dialog box.

Step 6: Formatting Page Layout with Tables, Layers, and Frames

Tables, layers, and frames are all used to control page layout. Tables divide your page into a grid of rows and columns, and they allow you to place blocks of text, images, or other content (such as video) in a *cell* at the intersection of a row and a column. Layers are more flexible than tables in that they can be placed anywhere on a page. Frames combine two or more web pages into a *frameset*—which appears to be one page in a visitor's browser. Framesets are often used to place a static navigation page in one frame and changing content in another frame.

One frequently used and effective technique in page design is to use a single-cell (one column, one row) table to define your page size. When you define page width, either in percent or pixels, you can constrain your page content so it does not expand to fill the width of a browser window, but instead conforms to a set size. Constraining page content in a table produces content that will be more consistent in different viewing environments, as demonstrated in Figure 6-13.

Figure 6-13
On top, a web page without tables; on the bottom, the same content with the page width constrained by a table

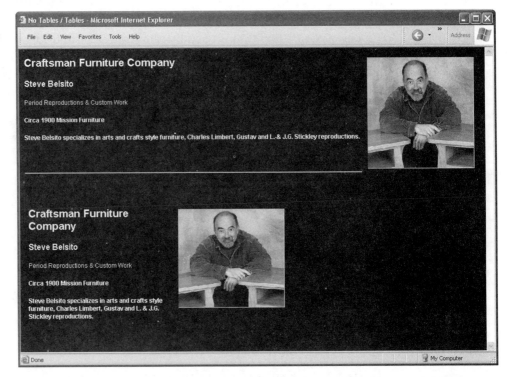

To create a single-cell table to constrain your page content, choose Insert | Table. In the Insert Table dialog box, enter 1 row and 1 column. In the Width box, enter the size to which you want to constrain your page width. *Spacing* is the space *between cells* and is normally not useful in a one-cell table. Table *padding* is the *buffer space* between cell content and the edge of a cell. You should start by setting cell padding at 6 pixels. You can change this at any time in the Properties inspector for a selected table.

How Wide Should Your Page Be?

Page width is often set to 780 pixels. This creates a page that will display without horizontal scrolling in most monitors. Pixels provide a fixed size for your table, while percentage creates a table whose size changes relative to the width of a visitor's browser window:

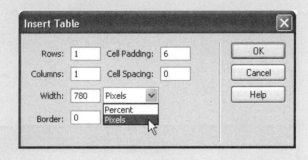

After you define a table, you can edit it using the Properties inspector. To select a table for editing, click in its upper-left corner or click the <table> element tag that appears on the bottom of the page.

Tables can be aligned left, right, or center, allowing text to flow around them. Table borders can be set by entering a value (in pixels) in the Border box of the Properties inspector. Table Background Color sets a color for the background of the entire table. The Brdr Color box allows you to choose a color of the border around the table (if there is one). You can tile an image across the back of an entire table using the Background Image box to navigate to an image file.

Another, more complex, technique is to create tables with several columns, and use them to lay out text in newspaper-like vertical strips, as you can see in Figure 6-14.

Figure 6-14
Laying out a
page with a three
column table

The most complex technique for page design with tables is to create tables with multiple rows and columns and use cells to hold content. You can merge *contiguous* (connected) cells by clicking and dragging to select them, and then clicking the Merge Cells button in the Properties inspector. You can resize rows or columns simply by clicking and dragging on the dividers between them:

Web Text Doesn't Flow Between Columns

If you make a two-column table and then add text to it, don't assume that the text will automatically "flow" into the second column. That works in your word processor or your desktop publishing program, but unfortunately it doesn't work in web tables. You must use the Properties inspector to link the columns.

In addition to formatting table properties, you can define custom background colors, vertical alignment, and other features for individual cells. When you click in a table cell, the Properties inspector shows properties for the cell content on top (for instance, for the text in a cell) and cell properties on the bottom. By default, cell content is centered vertically, so if you want to make the content line up at the top of a cell, you need to reset the vertical alignment to Top using the Vert drop-down list in the cell Properties inspector.

Layers can be any size, and they can be placed anywhere on a page. They are not quite as reliable as tables when viewed in older browsers or unconventional browsers, but they're reliable enough to use in most sites.

To place a layer on your page, choose Insert | Layer. Click and drag the handle in the upper-left corner of the layer to move it. You can resize a selected layer by clicking and dragging a side, top, or corner handle.

Once you create a layer, you can enter text, place an image, or place any other page object inside that layer:

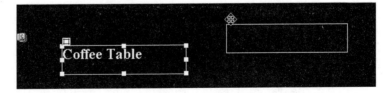

Overlapping Layers Are Not Reliable

While layers are pretty reliable for displaying content, overlapping layers can be problematic with many browsers. To avoid having your layers overlap, choose Window | Others | Layers, and click the Prevent Overlaps checkbox in the Layers inspector. For the ultimate in stability, choose Modify | Convert | Tables to Layers. Accept the default settings in the Convert Layers to Table dialog box and click OK to convert your layers to tables.

If you want to use a frameset to create a combination of an embedded navigation frame (or two navigation frames), the best way to do this is to take
advantage of Dreamweaver's full set of frame templates. Choose File | New, and
then click Framesets in the Category list of the New Document dialog box,
shown in Figure 6-15. Choose a frameset option, and examine the Preview area
to see how that frameset will look. Unless you are comfortable with framesets,
it's best to avoid *nested* framesets that make design more complex than simple
framesets. With a frameset template selected, click Create to generate a frameset
page.

Figure 6-15
Creating a frameset
from a template

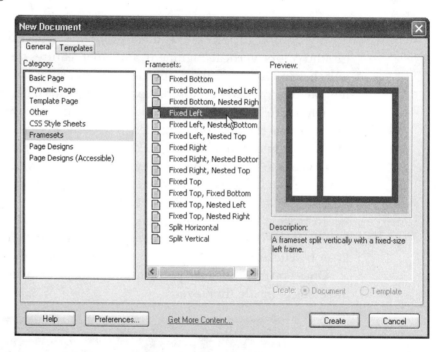

The frameset you generate will actually embed at least three HTML (web)
pages. The first page will not have any content but will simply define the layout
of the frameset itself. Other web pages will be embedded inside this frameset. To
resize the border between your frames, click and drag the divider.

Choose Window | Others | Frames to display the Frames inspector. Here,
you can define the kind of border to display between frames (if any) along with
other frameset properties. Click one of your embedded frame pages in the
Frames inspector to activate the Properties inspector for that frame. If you want
to allow scrollbars in a selected frame, leave the Scroll drop-down list set to the

default of Auto. If you want to prohibit scrollbars in a selected frame, choose No from the drop-down list.

Click the No Resize checkbox to prevent visitors from changing the border between your frames in their browsers. Set Borders to No for a clean, borderless look (no border will be visible between your frames). See Figure 6-16.

Figure 6-16
Defining a frame without resizable borders, with no scrollbar permitted, and with no visible border

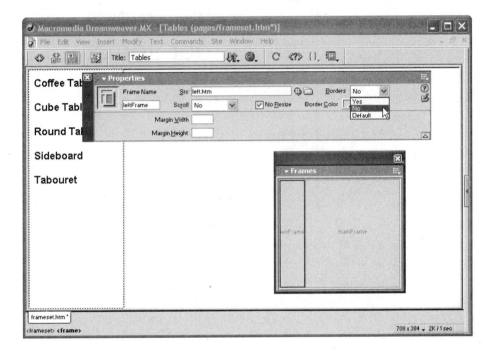

Click inside an embedded page to enter content into that page. After you've entered content in both of your embedded pages, choose File | Save All to save all the open web pages in your frameset. The Save As dialog box will appear repeatedly, allowing you to save each of your embedded framed pages. You can tell which page you are saving by the gray dashed line that appears around a page as you save your pages.

There is a special trick for using links in frames. You must tell a link in *which frame* it should open. Typically, a left or top frame will be used as a navigation frame. Links launched from a navigation frame normally do *not* open in the frame (web page) from which they are launched. Instead, links in a navigation frame open in what is called the *main frame*. Both frames are shown in Figure 6-17.

Figure 6-17
(Left) navigation
frame and (right)
main frame

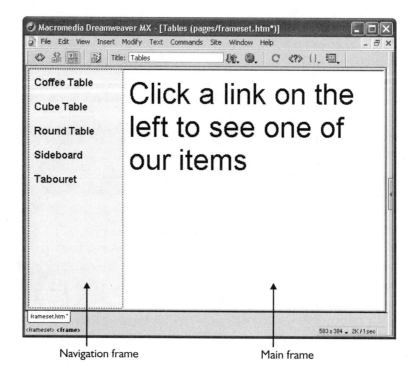

Navigation frame   Main frame

When you define a link in a navigation frame, use the Target drop-down list in the Properties inspector to open the link in the main frame.

Test Your Links!

Be sure to test all the links in your frameset to make sure they open in the correct frame. If a link opens in the incorrect frame—for instance in the navigation frame instead of the main frame—recheck your link target settings, as shown here. As long as you generate framesets from one of Dreamweaver's template pages, as described in Step 6, target frames will be available in the Target drop-down list of the Properties inspector. If you don't see an option to set the target to the main frame, redo your frameset using one of the frame template pages.

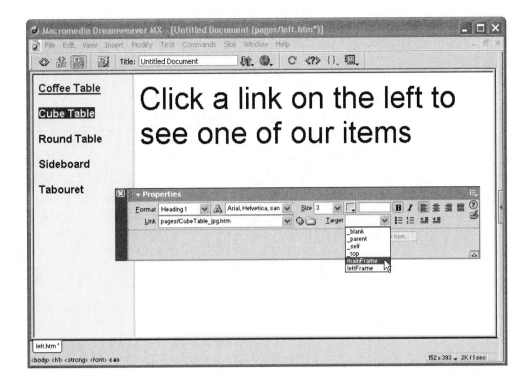

Step 7: Uploading Your Web Pages in the Site Window

After you have developed your web site on your local computer (at your home or office), you can *upload* (send) your site content to a remote server so it can be accessed on the Internet. To do this, you must already have a web host provider and a domain name (or some kind of URL). You'll also need login information that is provided by your web hosting service.

If you don't have a web hosting service for your site, jump back to Chapter 2 for instructions on how to get one. If you do have a web hosting service, use Table 6-1 to make sure you have all the information you will need to log in to your site with Dreamweaver. Feel free to copy the list, and fill it out when you talk to your web host provider.

What You Need...	✔
URL—your web site domain name	☐
Type of access (normally FTP)	☐
FTP host address (make sure you get the *exact* information to enter when Dreamweaver asks for your FTP Host)	☐

Table 6-1
Info Checklist to Log in to Your Web Site

What You Need...	✔
Host director (some web hosts require additional host info, but most do not)	☐
Login (your login name to access your site)	☐
Password (the password you need to log in to your site)	☐

Table 6-1
Info Checklist to Log in to Your Web Site *(continued)*

Once you have filled out Table 6-1 with information provided by your web hosting service, expand the Site panel. With the Site panel expanded, choose Site | Edit Sites.

Select your site (the one you defined back in Step 1), and click the Edit button in the Define Sites dialog box. The Edit Sites dialog box appears. Click to select the name of the site you want, and click the Edit button. The Site Definition dialog box for your site opens. The Site Definition dialog box includes a list of categories along the left side. Start by selecting the Local Info category. Enter your URL in the HTTP Address area of the Local Info dialog box, as shown in Figure 6-18.

Figure 6-18
Defining your URL in the Site Definition dialog box

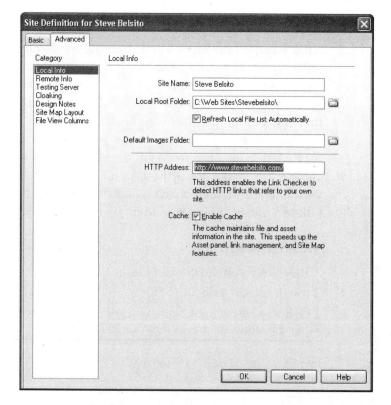

Next, select the Remote Info category from the Category list on the left side of the dialog box, as shown in Figure 6-19. In the Access drop-down list, select FTP. Type the FTP address (for example, ftp.webpage.com) in the FTP Host box. In the Login box, enter the username provided by your web hosting service. In the Password box, type the password given to you by your web hosting service. Finally, click OK when you've finished defining your remote hookup information.

Figure 6-19
Defining your
remote (upload)
connection settings

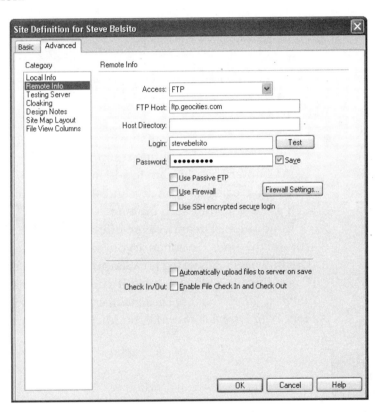

After you define your remote info, click Done to close the Edit Sites dialog box and return to the site menu. Now you're ready to send your files to your server.

You can upload all the files from your local site to your remote site by selecting your root local folder and choosing Site | Put. Later, as you edit files, you can click to select one file (or SHIFT-click to select many), and then choose Site | Put. Dreamweaver will establish a connection to your remote site. You'll be prompted to click OK to upload your entire site—do that to transfer files to your remote server. Now you can type in your web site's URL on the Internet and see your site. You're on the web, and ready for business.

Server Won't Accept Your Files?

If you run into problems sending files to your server, start by making sure you have an open Internet connection. Then go back over the information in the Site Definition dialog box—it's easy to make a small mistake in typing your URL, FTP address, login name, or password, and any error will disrupt your connection. Finally, if your Internet connection is working and your login information has been entered correctly, check with your web hosting service to determine why you can't connect to your site.

Step 8: Exploring More Features for Your Dreamweaver Web Site

In addition to features available in Dreamweaver, you can add features to your site by using available online resources.

In Chapter 7, you'll learn to add input forms to build a managed, online mailing list; to create an interactive guestbook; and to create and use other features such as a search box for your site.

In addition, Dreamweaver offers advanced features that are beyond the scope of this book. To enhance your site with animation and interactive *behaviors* (Dreamweaver generated JavaScript), or to apply enhanced formatting with *CSS* (Cascading Style Sheets), consult a dedicated book on Dreamweaver such as the *Complete Idiot's Guide to Dreamweaver MX*, by David Karlins, or *How To Do Everything With Dreamweaver MX*, by Michael Meadhra.

TESTING 1-2-3

Before you connect...

❏ The first step in creating a web site in Dreamweaver is to design your pages and save them to your local site on your own computer. Only after you have created and previewed your site locally are you ready to send your files to a remote server.

❏ Before you use the Dreamweaver site panel to upload (put) your files to your server, you will need login information provided by your web host administrator. You can minimize frustration and problems connecting to your remote site by using the checklist in this chapter to make sure you have all the information you'll need from your web server provider to connect to your remote web site.

Chapter 7

Enhancing Your Web Site with Server-Side Interactivity

Tools of the Trade

To add hit counters, sign-up forms, search boxes, guestbooks, and other server-based interactivity to your site, you'll first need to create a web site using the steps outlined in the previous chapters in this book. (Don't start the procedures in this chapter until you already have a functioning web site.) In addition to your web site, you'll need a connection to the Internet to access web sites that provide the server-based programs explored in this chapter.

In the previous chapters in this book, nearly all the elements you've added to your web site have one thing in common: the content you put on your web pages is transmitted to your visitors through the interaction of your visitor's *web browser* with your site content. To break that down a bit, most of the content on your site is translated into HTML (HyperText Markup Language) by programs such as PageBuilder, FrontPage, and Dreamweaver. These programs also generate other coding, such as JavaScript or DHTML (dynamic HTML), that allow objects to move around on your page or to react to a visitor's mouse movements.

On the visitor's end, browsers such as Internet Explorer interpret the formatting you assigned and the animation and interactivity you generated, and presto—visitors see text, images, media, and other elements the way you designed them on your pages. In some cases, additional software—such as a media plug-in—is necessary to interpret your web content. This software is installed on your *visitor's* computer. Because all this content is managed by software on the viewer's computer, you can also view your web pages and see all the elements in them on your computer, even before you upload your files to a web server.

You can add other, more powerful, elements to your web site that add another level of interactivity between your site and its visitors. These dynamic and interactive page elements use programs installed on a *server* to manage online databases that provide ever-changing content on your web pages.

A few examples of this *server-side* content are search boxes that look up text and provide visitors with a list of relevant links, page counters that tell you how many people have visited your web site, and mailing lists that allow visitors to sign up (or be removed from) your e-mail list. (See Figure 7-1.)

Figure 7-1
Joining an online
e-mail list

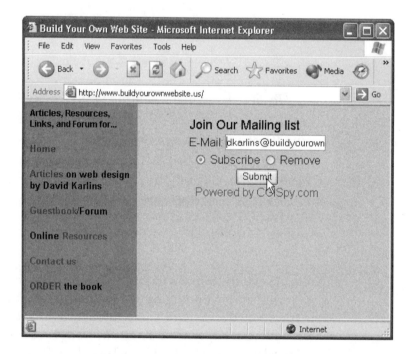

Page elements such as a page counter, an e-mail list, or a search box rely on content that is *managed* on a *web server*. A page counter reflects information saved at your web server that records the number of *hits* (visits) received by your site. An interactive e-mail list stores e-mail addresses in a database that is *updated* and *managed* on your *web server*. And a search box, like the one shown in Figure 7-2, relies on an updatable index of your web site that is saved in a file—again, *managed* by software on your *web server*.

Figure 7-2
Results of a search are displayed on a page at a server.

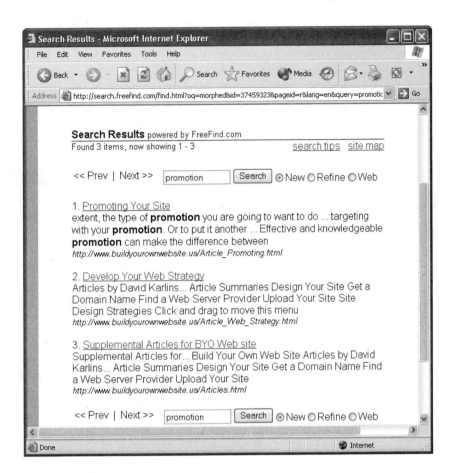

To summarize, web page elements that rely on content that is processed entirely in a browser (or with plug-ins) is referred to as *client-side* content, while content that is processed on a server is called, somewhat intuitively, *server-side* content. In this chapter, you'll learn to place elements on your web pages that utilize *server-side* content.

Content that is sent to a server is often collected in a *form*. Forms are special areas of a web site with input fields (such as text boxes, checkboxes, or a submit button). HTML code associated with your form directs the information that is collected to a server, where the information is processed, frequently added to a database of some type, and then sometimes redirected to a web page, an e-mail address, or even an interactive online graph.

Where do you get this server-side code? If you have the resources, you hire a programmer or a team of programmers to create custom server-side programs (written in programming languages like Perl). If you have a modest budget, such as that of a small company or large nonprofit, you can contract for web server space with a provider that includes server-side scripts (programs) as part of its web hosting process. PageBuilder, Dreamweaver, and FrontPage all provide form-building tools that can be used to design the *front end* of server connections—that is, the interface that visitors will use, such as the one shown in Figure 7-3, to submit information to a server. However, these forms are useless without server-side scripts to which they connect.

Figure 7-3
Submitting information to a server

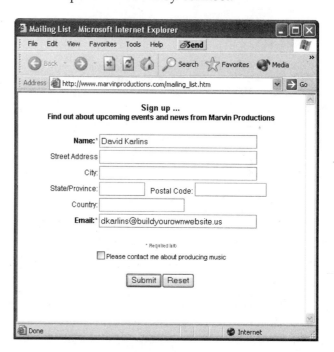

Advanced Options...

Dreamweaver and FrontPage provide tools for generating server-side scripting, but those tools are the advanced edge of those products and are beyond the scope of this book.

The easiest way to embed server-side objects on your web pages is to avail yourself of the many online sites that provide turnkey server-side objects that are hosted on their servers. This means that some of your web site content (for example, your e-mail mailing list, the index of your site used by a search engine, or a statistical analysis of who is visiting your site and when) is not going to be saved on the server that hosts your web site, but instead will be saved on the server of the company providing the server-side elements. Many online sites, including those discussed in this chapter, provide scripts and server hosting for free. Others have a "for free" option that requires the inclusion of advertising, or they charge for ad-free sites.

These online server resources allow developers on a limited budget or those who lack access to server programming expertise to utilize interactive server-side objects on their web pages. Even if your web host provides server scripting, you'll find the steps in this chapter will teach you techniques that can be used to embed server-side content in your pages, regardless of the source.

The Common Gateway Interface (CGI) scripts covered in this chapter are elements that many, if not most, sites can use. Feel free, of course, to skip elements you don't think are appropriate to your site. After you install at least a few of the CGI script elements discussed in this chapter, you'll be prepared to hunt around for additional CGI scripts or to work with a web host provider or programmer who develops custom CGI scripts for you.

Finally, before you begin to add CGI scripts to your site, you'll need to know how to integrate them using PageBuilder, FrontPage, or Dreamweaver. The sites that provide CGI scripts generate HTML code for your page that links your CGI elements to scripts at the server. You'll need to copy this HTML code into your operating system clipboard, and then paste it into your web page.

To paste copied HTML code into a Dreamweaver web page, choose Edit | Paste HTML. In Dreamweaver's Design view (the default, WYSIWG way of looking at pages in Dreamweaver), the code you paste will appear as page *objects*—forms that collect e-mail addresses, search text, and so on.

With FrontPage, the process varies a bit, depending on which version you are using. In FrontPage 2000 and FrontPage 2002, you can choose Edit | Paste Special, and then choose the Treat As HTML option.

With PageBuilder, choose Insert | Forms And Scripts | HTML Code, and then paste the HTML code provided by the CGI script host into the Script Properties dialog box. When you click OK to close the Script Properties dialog box, the CGI element will appear in the PageBuilder window as an icon, but you can see your actual CGI object by clicking the Preview button.

Now that you understand how CGI scripts connect to forms on your page, and you're prepared to copy and paste HTML, you're ready to start adding interactive forms to your site.

Step 1: Adding a Search Box to Your Site

Search boxes help make the content of your site more accessible to visitors—which is a good thing! Another, less appreciated value of including a search box on your web site is that most search engines provide periodic reports on who is searching for what at your site, as shown in Figure 7-4. These reports generated from your search box are one of the most valuable ways of monitoring who is coming to your site and what site content visitors are requesting.

Figure 7-4
Studying a search report to learn what visitors are looking for at your site

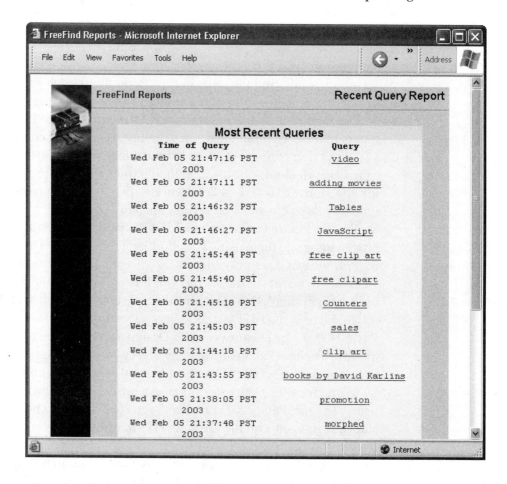

In general, search boxes provided by servers furnish three options—you can allow visitors to search *your site*, you can allow visitors to search the *whole* web, or you can allow a search on *both*.

Keep Searchers at Your *Site*

Search boxes that provide listings from the entire Internet might be valuable to visitors, but they have the drawback of diverting visitors *away* from your site, when you probably want them to stay put.

Search boxes that work for your site are based on a periodically regenerated *index* file that lists all the (text) content in your web pages, along with links to the page that contains each *string* (block) of text. You can tell the server how often you want your site reindexed. Sites that change content daily need to be reindexed frequently, while those that have fairly static content need not be reindexed often.

Search boxes also provide various options regarding what information is listed in the results display. Some search engines allow you to list quite a bit of information about pages, while others simply list links. The search box you will learn to use here comes from FreeFind (*www.freefind.com*). The FreeFind search engine provides reports to help you monitor the topics being searched for at your site. The instructions that follow will show you how to add the free version, but the steps are similar for installing the professional version.

1. Browse to *www.freefind.com*. You'll find a sign-up form and the option of getting the free version or the professional (paid, ad-free) version. After you fill out the two fields in the sign-up form (your URL and e-mail address), click Instant Sign-up, as shown in Figure 7-5.

Figure 7-5
Signing up for
a search box at
FreeFind.com

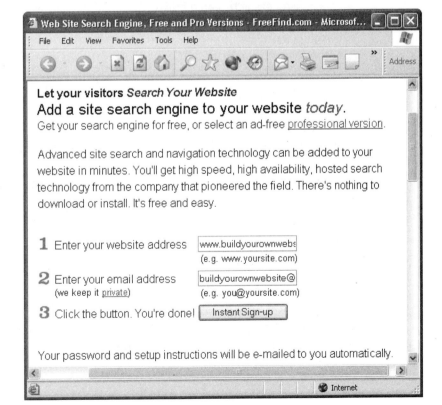

2. After you sign up for a FreeFind account, a site ID number and password are sent to your e-mail address. Check your e-mail (it doesn't take long). When you have your site ID and password, click the Login link at the FreeFind.com web site.

3. The first time you log in, you'll be prompted to select a type of account. Feel free to start with a free account—you can always upgrade later if you find you need more features.

4. After you select a type of account, you'll jump to an instant setup page. Here, you'll do two things that will enable your search box to work: you'll have the search engine at FreeFind index (make a list of all the words in) your web site, and you'll generate HTML code that will place the search box on your web page.

5. To index your site, click the Build Index link (a tab link at the top of the page). The first link on the Build Index page searches your site and generates a database listing all the words in your site. You can click the Index link now to generate a searchable database of words on your site. After FreeFind indexes your site, you'll get an e-mail telling you the process is finished.

By default, the FreeFind *spider* search program goes to your index page. It then follows links from that page to search additional pages. If all the pages on your site are linked to your home page, or they're linked to pages that link to your home page, you don't need to worry about the Set Starting Point feature. But if you want to include pages in your search results that are *not* linked to your home page, you can use the Set Starting Point link to list the full URL of pages that are not linked to your home page and include them in the search results.

Every time your site content changes, your search index becomes outdated. Most web designers don't reindex every time a minor change is made, but you will want to schedule automatic reindexing using a time interval that's appropriate to how often your content changes. A considerate webmaster will update the search index after deleting or renaming pages; otherwise, the search results will display corrupted links in the results list.

Click the Schedule Re-indexing link at the Build Index tab at the Freefind web site to define how often you want your site indexed. Use the form shown in Figure 7-6 to choose how often you want your site reindexed, and choose a time (and time zone) when indexing will not interfere with peak traffic at your site.

Figure 7-6
Setting up automatic reindexing

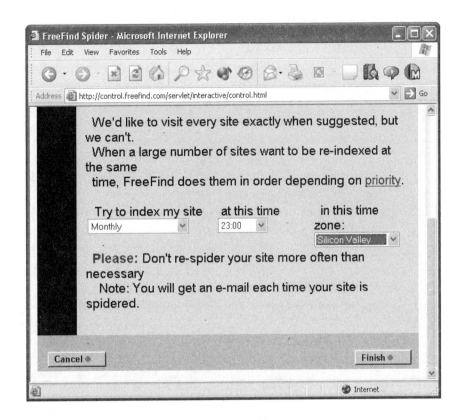

HEADS UP!

Don't Overschedule Indexing

Don't schedule reindexing more often than needed. If the FreeFind search engine finds that nothing has changed between indexing sessions, you'll be automatically dropped from the service.

If for some reason you don't want some content on a page included in a search results list, click the Exclude Pages option and add pages to the list.

The FreeFind search engine will even go through PDF (Portable Document Format) files and include them in search results. If you want to include PDF files in your search results, click the PDF Indexing link. This valuable feature is included with paid accounts only.

The Define Subsections option in the Advanced area of the Build Index page is not something small businesses and organizations are likely to need. The Password Protected Areas feature applies only to sites where a server host provides pages protected by passwords. Often, the content on these pages is not something you want to show up in a search engine list.

If you used the Frames design features in either FrontPage or Dreamweaver, and you are placing your search box in a navigation frame, you can use the Result Link Target feature to define the frame target in which to display results. For example, if you used the steps in this book to build a frameset in Dreamweaver, and you are placing a search box in the left navigation frame, you'll want to enter **http://*www.yoururl.ext*/mainframe** in the text area box in the Result Link Targets page (substituting your own URL for *www.yoururl.ext*).

After you have generated an index for your site and defined any indexing options you need, you can place a search box on your page. Use the HTML link (from the tabbed links on top of the page) to navigate to a set of search boxes. Some of the search boxes include radio buttons that allow visitors to choose between searching your site and searching the web. Other search boxes allow visitors to search your site, as shown in Figure 7-7, *or* the web. Finally, at the end of the page, you'll find HTML code that generates links to an automatically generated site map or to a list of new pages on your site. Find a search box you like, and then copy the associated HTML to your operating system clipboard.

Figure 7-7
Choosing a search box to search just your web site

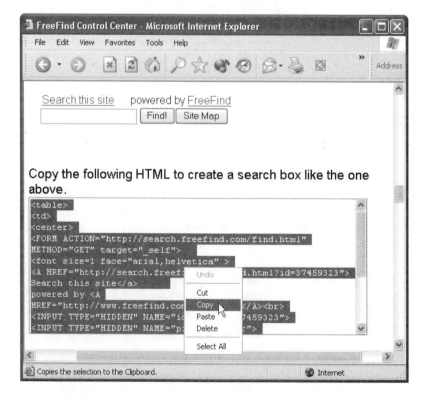

With the HTML for your search box copied into your clipboard, open the page in your web site where the search box will be located, using your web design software. Then follow the instructions for pasting HTML into a web page, which were detailed for PageBuilder, FrontPage, and Dreamweaver at the beginning of this chapter. See Figure 7-8.

Figure 7-8
Pasting HTML code
for a search box into
PageBuilder

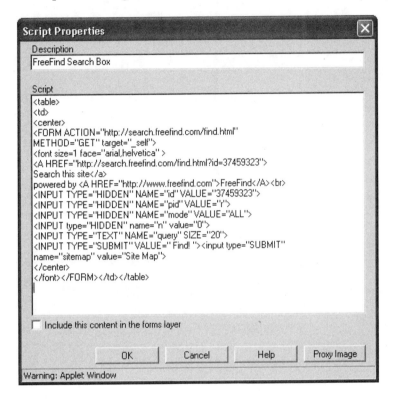

After you paste the HTML code into your web page editor, you can preview and test it by previewing your page in a web browser. In FrontPage, you can use the Preview tab in the Page/Design view; in PageBuilder, click the Preview icon at the top of the screen; and in Dreamweaver, choose File | Preview In Browser to see your form in a browser.

You can view your page in a browser to test the search box. Try searching for text for which you anticipate visitors might search:

Make Your Page Content Search-Friendly

If you find that words or phrases for which you anticipate visitors will search don't produce any results pages, revisit the content in your pages and revise it to include the phrases or words you think visitors will be looking for.

To test your search box in a browser, enter a word or phrase, click the Find button, and examine the results. The results appear in a page at the FreeFind server, as shown in Figure 7-9. If visitors click a link in the list of search results, they'll *return* to a page at your site. If visitors don't follow any of the generated links (or if their search doesn't yield any matches), they will have to click the Back button in their browser to return to your site. Alternatively, you can add a link back to your web site by choosing the Link Back Text feature on the Customize page at FreeFind.

Figure 7-9
FreeFind search
results displayed
for visitors

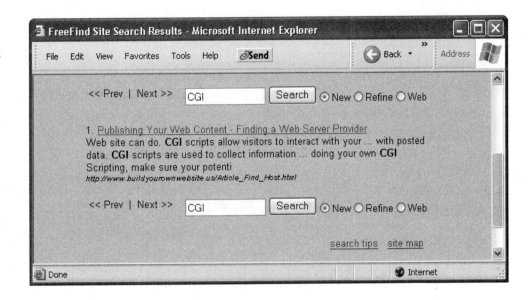

Other features available at the Customize page at FreeFind include options to change the page properties of the search results page. Use these features to match the background color, text color, and other formatting elements of your search results page with the pages at your web site. This will integrate the results page with the look and feel of your own site. Still more features at the Customize page allow you to tweak how search results are produced and displayed.

Step 2: Setting Up and Managing an E-mail List

Rare is the web site that can't benefit from collecting a mailing list of interested visitors—for example, small businesses can send out directed mailings to customers who want to get e-mail, nonprofits can build donor lists, and organizations can sign up members.

A free sign-up list available from CGISpy (*www.cgispy.com*) lets visitors sign up or get removed from your e-mail list. Features available at the CGISpy site allow you to send out e-mails to the list or delete folks from the list.

As with other CGI providers, CGISpy requires that you register before you can use its scripts. Go to *www.cgispy.com* and click the Signup link. After you complete the sign-up form, click the link to log in. Use the username and password you assigned yourself to log in to the set of CGI scripts available at CGISpy, as shown in Figure 7-10.

Figure 7-10
CGI scripts available
at CGISpy

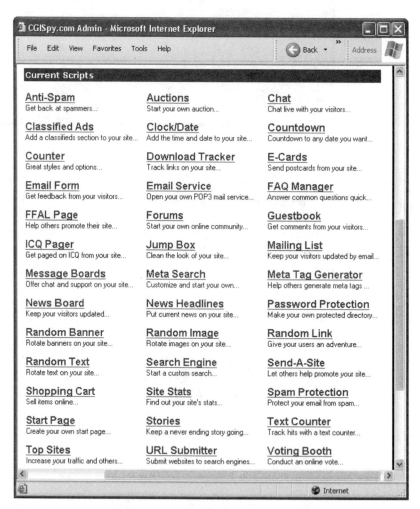

Many of the listed CGI scripts are available to paying subscribers only. However, some of the most useful scripts are free, including one that allows you to include an e-mail sign-up form on your page. Click the Mailing List link on the CGISpy Main Admin page to access the Mailing List Administration page at CGISpy.

The Mailing List Administration page has several links to features that are used to administer your mailing list once it is set up. The E-Mail List Code link allows you to remove e-mail addresses from your list. The Send E-Mail To Mailing List link lets you enter e-mail content and send that to everyone on your list. The helpful Backup Your List link downloads a copy of your mailing list, which you can then manage with your own e-mail software.

The Edit E-Mail List Header and Edit E-Mail List Footer links allow you to change the content of the header information at the top of e-mails and footer information at the bottom of e-mails, but these features require that you enter (or paste) HTML code. Finally, the Thank You Message link lets you define the message that appears when people join your mailing list. However, none of these features are essential for collecting e-mails from visitors.

Click the E-Mail List Code link to access the page that contains the code for your sign-up form. Use the Copy To Clipboard button to copy the code to the clipboard.

Use the instructions in the first part of this chapter (the instructions that appear prior to Step 1) to paste the copied HTML into your web design program, as shown in Figure 7-11.

Figure 7-11
Copying HTML for a mailing list sign-up form

You can use the text formatting features in FrontPage or Dreamweaver to touch up the formatting of the text in the sign-up form, as shown in Figure 7-12.

Figure 7-12
Formatting your
sign-up form in
Dreamweaver

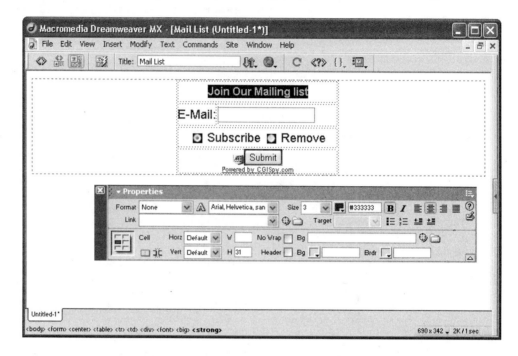

You'll want to test your form features—both the sign-up and remove features.

As visitors sign up for your mailing list, you can administer the list. Do that by logging in at CGISpy and clicking on the Mailing List link to open the Mailing List Administration page. To send an e-mail to your list, click the Send E-Mail To Mailing List link. As shown in Figure 7-13, enter a subject and a message, and then click Send Mails to send the e-mail to everyone on your list.

Figure 7-13
Sending out an
e-mail to your
online mailing list

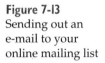

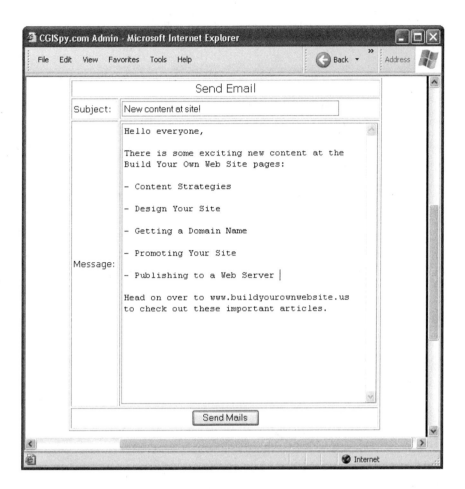

Figure 7-13
Sending out an
e-mail to your
online mailing list

Step 3: Setting Up a Guestbook

Guestbooks allow visitors to post their own content to your web site. They are part of a larger family of web pages that allow visitors to post content. A *blog* (short for web log) can be used to post periodic writings on any topic. *Threaded discussion forums* host discussions on multiple topics to which visitors can contribute. All these types of pages allow visitors to add content to your web site.

There are many good reasons for including a guestbook or some other form of interactive page on your site. Guestbooks make visitors feel a part of your site. In addition, a guestbook is a source of content for your site—content that *you* don't have to create.

Obviously guestbooks, blogs, and discussion forums usually require a moderator. After all, as the host of an interactive page, you will probably want and need to take some responsibility for the content posted at your site. That doesn't mean that you need to exercise a heavy hand of censorship, but you do need some way of editing or deleting inappropriate content when necessary.

The guestbook CGI script you'll use in this step is from CGISpy and provides options that allow you to see and approve content before it is posted. The program also has an optional feature that substitutes @#$% for "bad" words.

To access the CGI script for a guestbook, log in to CGISpy (*www.cgispy.com*) using the password and user ID you were given when you signed up earlier. If you haven't signed up for a (free) CGISpy membership, do this first.

From the list of links to CGI scripts on the CGISpy home page, choose the Guestbook link. The Guestbook Administration page provides five links to create, edit, and manage your guestbook. The Edit GuestBook link allows you to change both the page formatting of your guestbook web page and some of the rules for your guestbook (for example, if you want to approve postings in advance, or if you want to filter for bad words).

The Edit GuestBook Header and Edit GuestBook Footer links allow you to change the content of the top and bottom of the guestbook page, respectively.

The options you select in the Edit Guestbook, Edit Guestbook Header, and Edit Guestbook Footer pages will change how your guestbook will look and will change the code that CGISpy generates for your guestbook. Follow these links and customize your pages *before* you copy and paste the guestbook code.

You'll use the Delete Posts From Your Guestbook link only after folks have started posting to your site. At that point, you can use this link to edit the contents of the guestbook.

The first five options at the Edit Guestbook link format the color of your text, (unvisited) links, and background color or link. For a professional look, you'll want these colors (or background images for your page) to match the formatting of the web pages at your site—see Figure 7-14. This way, visitors' trips to the guestbook will be seamless, and it won't be obvious to them that they have actually left your site and your server for a page at another server. Click the question mark (?) link next to each option for quick access to a palette of web-safe colors, along with the six-digit code associated with each color.

Figure 7-14
Configuring colors for your guestbook to match the color scheme on your own web pages

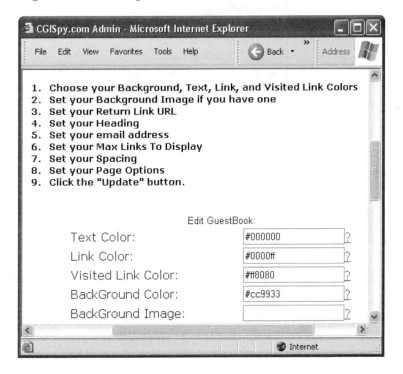

The remaining options on the Edit Guestbook page, most of which are shown in Figure 7-15, allow you to define how the page will work. The Return Link field defines the link that visitors will follow to return to your web site. You can make this a link to your home page or to any page at your site. The Heading field defines the message at the top of the guestbook. The Max Display field determines how many postings can be displayed on a page, and the Separate Type box lets you choose how additional postings will be displayed, either on a new page (Page Break) or separated by a line (Horizontal Line).

Figure 7-15
Defining how
your guestbook
will operate

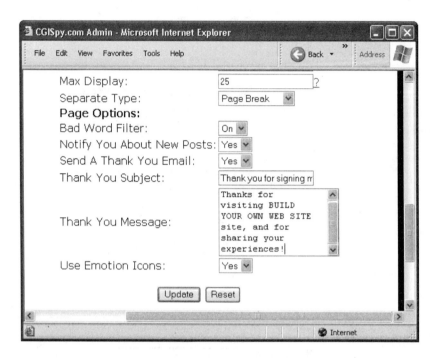

The Bad Word Filter changes bad words to characters (@#$%). The Notify You About New Posts option is an important one. You'll almost always want to choose Yes for this option, so you can be aware of postings before they appear on the guestbook page.

If you select Yes for the Send A Thank You Email option, you can define a Thank You Subject line and a Thank You Message for the e-mails that people get if they post to the site.

Finally, the Use Emotion Icons field allows visitors to post a happy face, wink, frown, and other icons in addition to text submissions.

After you've defined the format and options for your guestbook, click Update to generate the HTML code with the options and formatting you chose.

The Edit Guestbook Header and Edit Guestbook Footer links take you to screens where you can create additional content for the guestbook page that will appear at the header or footer of the guestbook. This content is not required. Unfortunately, CGISpy expects you to be able to enter your own HTML in these screens if you want to include formatting or images.

HTML for Non-Coders

Even if you don't know how to write code using HTML, you can experiment by using the HTML tab in FrontPage or the Code view in Dreamweaver to copy and paste HTML into the Edit Guestbook Header and Edit GuestBook Footer pages, as shown in Figure 7-16. Do this by formatting or editing your text in the Normal view in FrontPage, or in Design view in Dreamweaver, and then switch to HTML view in FrontPage or Code view in Dreamweaver, and copy the HTML you generated. Paste that HTML into the Edit Guestbook Header or Edit Guestbook Footer page at CGISpy.

Figure 7-16
If you know a little HTML, or if you can fake a few lines, you can add content to the page header for your guestbook page.

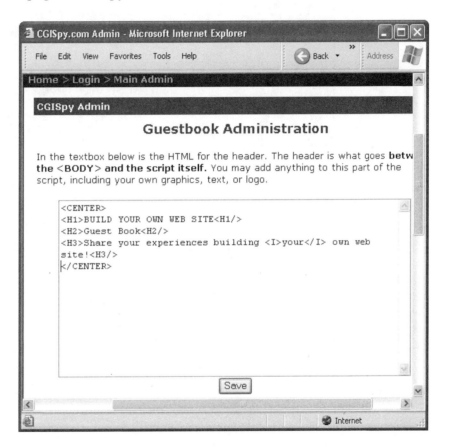

After you've customized your guestbook, you're ready to copy the URL provided by CGISpy at the main Guestbook Administration page and link to that page from your own web site. Your link will begin *http://scripts.cgispy.com/ guestbook.cgi?a=view&user=*, and it will end with your own CGISpy ID. This *entire link* is generated for you at the Guestbook Administration page, so you simply copy it to your clipboard.

Finally, create a link at your own web site to the guestbook. If you formatted your page with similar colors to those in your web site, visitors won't feel like they've left your site to fill out your guestbook form. Your page may look similar to the one shown in Figure 7-17.

Figure 7-17
This guestbook form opens in a framed page so it appears to be integrated tightly into the rest of the site.

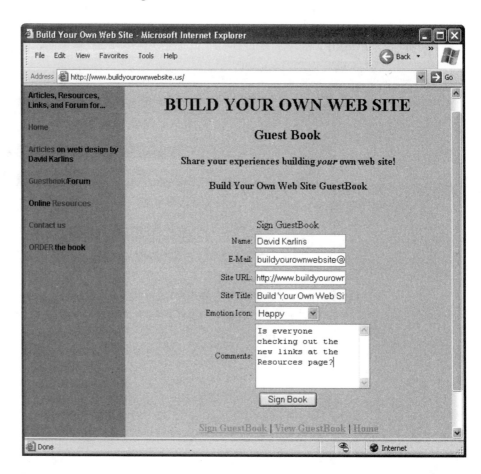

TIPS OF THE TRADE

Embedding Forms in a Frameset

You can embed your guestbook form and the guestbook itself in a frameset using the frame features covered in the Dreamweaver (Chapter 6) section in this book.

You can administer your guestbook by logging into CGISpy and following the Guestbook link. In the Guestbook Administration page, click the Edit Guestbook Entries link, and use the checkboxes on the Delete Guestbook Entries page to mark postings for deletion. Click the Delete Entries button to zap the unwanted postings from your guestbook.

Figure 7-18
Viewing postings at the guestbook—the "bad" word filter is in effect

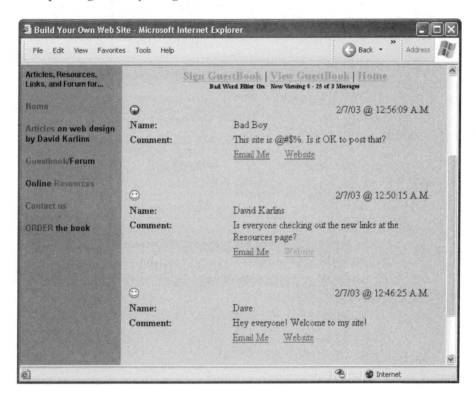

Now that you have your own guestbook, feel free to post a link to it at the book's web site (*www.buildyourownwebsite.us*) so other readers can post commentary like that shown in Figure 7-18 at your web site.

Step 4: Giving Directions

It's easy to provide visitors to your web site with an interactive map and directions to your office or location. Here, we'll use the easy-to-access Yahoo! Maps (*http://maps.yahoo.com/*) server to provide maps and links.

Start by going to Yahoo! Maps (*http://maps.yahoo.com/*), as shown here.

In the Address area, enter the street address including the city, state, and zip code (if in the United States) of the location you want to map, and click the Get Map link. The link in the address line of your browser locates the map you just generated. That link is long! But you can copy and paste it by clicking in the address line of your browser and copying the entire URL to your clipboard.

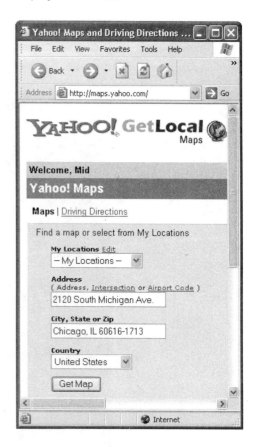

Then create a link at your web site to the directions page. If your visitors have defined a "My Location" at Yahoo!, they'll automatically be able to look up driving directions from their location to yours. Otherwise, visitors can still follow a link to generate directions to your location, as shown in Figure 7-19.

Figure 7-19
Defining a link to
a Yahoo! Map

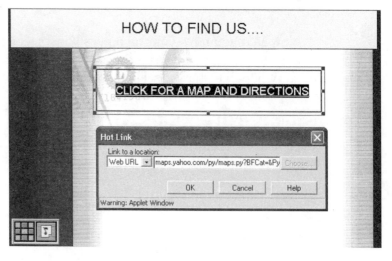

A location link is easy to define—the Yahoo! server does most of the work. Businesses and organizations that rely on folks being able to find their physical location will find that providing web visitors with quick and easy directions is a valuable feature at a web site.

Step 5: Polling Your Visitors

A number of CGI scripts are available at the Hosted Scripts site (*www.hostedscripts.com*). In general, these scripts are a bit more complex than those available from CGISpy, FreeFind, or linking to a Yahoo! Map. Many of them require that you do some editing of the HTML that you copy into your page design program (PageBuilder, FrontPage, or Dreamweaver). However, they provide more complex and powerful interactive forms than those available elsewhere.

The poll script is a fun way to let visitors interact with your site, and it does not require you to edit HTML. You create a question, supply a variety of answers, and let visitors vote. The results are posted and graphed (relatively) instantly at the server for visitors to see.

Like other providers of CGI scripts, Hosted Scripts requires that you register the first time you visit. Click the Sign Up! link and fill out the sign-up form to register; then click the Sign Up button to submit your registration info. Then use the User and Pass (for password) boxes on the top of the page to log in.

After you log in, click the Polls link on the left side of the page. Four links are available to use for creating a poll. The Add Poll link allows you to define a question and possible answers. The Delete Poll link removes a poll. Get HTML Codes generates HTML that provides a link to your poll.

Start by clicking the Add Poll link and entering a question in the box. Then choose a number of possible answers from the drop-down list shown in Figure 7-20.

Figure 7-20
Defining a question for your poll, and selecting a number of possible answers

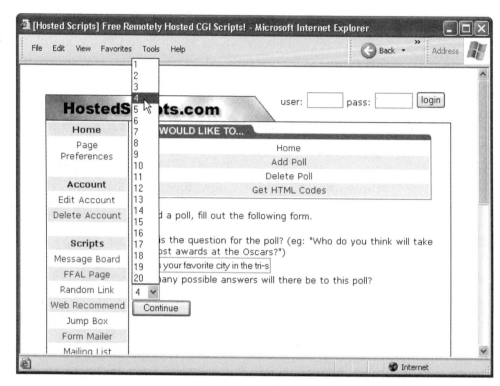

After you tell Hosted Scripts how many answers you'll be adding, click the Continue button and fill in possible answers in the boxes provided. Click the Continue button on this page to generate the script that will display your poll and the results.

Click the Get HTML Codes link, and copy the HTML that links to your poll into your site clipboard, as shown in Figure 7-21. Note that the script that manages this poll detects whether or not a visitor has already voted, and it will let visitors vote only once in your poll.

Figure 7-21
Copying HTML
to create a link to
your poll

The basic techniques you learned in this chapter can be applied to connect your pages to any other CGI scripts. Check with your web server provider to find out what CGI scripts are offered.

In addition, now that you've learned to generate and connect to CGI scripts, feel free to search for CGI scripts on the web or to contract with a programmer to create custom CGI scripts. The following table summarizes how to access the CGI scripts covered in this chapter and lists a couple others that you can explore as well.

Element	What It Does	Where You Get It
Search boxes	Connect to an index of your site at a server and provide a list of relevant links.	*www.freefind.com*

Element	What It Does	Where You Get It
Mail List Management	Allow visitors to add, and delete (and an administrator to edit) contact information stored in a database at a server.	*www.cgispy.com*
Directions	Allow visitors to see a map of your location and find directions to your location.	*http://maps.yahoo.com/*
Guest Book	Allow visitors to post comments and interact in discussion, and allow a moderator to edit site content.	*www.cgispy.com*
Password Protection	Restrict access to a page to visitors in a server-hosted database—allow administrator to add or delete authorized visitors.	*http://www.hostedscripts.com/*
Interactive Poll	Allow visitors to vote on an issue, and watch updated poll results online.	*http://www.hostedscripts.com/*

Part III

Keeping Your
Web Site Working
and Up to Date

Chapter 8

Placing Your Site on Search Engines

Tools of the Trade

In this chapter, you'll need your web editing software (PageBuilder, FrontPage, or Dreamweaver) and an Internet connection to access the sign-up pages for various search engines and directories.

Promoting Your Web Site

Once you've created a web site, you'll want to promote it. Getting visitors to your web site involves many dimensions of promotion. Visitors will find your site in one of three ways: they will hear about it from you, they'll follow a link from another site, or they'll find it using a search engine.

While offline promotion and advertising is often the most important part of promoting your web site, the key is to integrate promoting your web site into your company or organization's overall advertising and promotion strategy. The realm of advertising and promotion per se is beyond the scope of this book. However, this chapter will focus on how you can promote your site on the web itself by maximizing the hits generated by search engines.

The steps in this chapter will show you how to tweak the *content* of your web pages to make them more attractive to search engines, as well as how to get listed with the main search engines.

Getting the Whole Organization on Board

Many times, the web designer (or web design team) needs to do protracted education within an organization to plug people, departments, or resources into promoting the web site. For instance, brochures should promote your web site as a source of updated information. Your web site URL can be added to the company voice mail messages, and so on. It's important to unleash the creativity and initiative of your *entire organization* in promoting the web site and not leave it as the province of the web design team.

Your goal is to have your company, organization, or institution among the first ten or so listings that appear when a web surfer enters a phrase into a search box. For example, in Figure 8-1, a firm named Bard Consulting has configured its site so that when someone searches for "Bard Consulting" at Google, the company is listed first (and second).

Figure 8-1
The goal is to have your site listed in the top 10 when visitors search for a term relevant to your site.

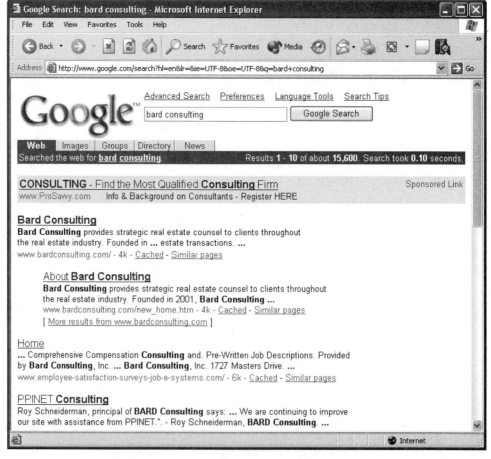

Having other sites link to your site is important in two ways: links from other sites generate traffic to your site, of course, but in addition, those links are often a trigger used to search engines to improve your listing in search results.

Other elements of web promotion include spreading the word about your site, creating attractive web content, and making your web site as *sticky* as possible, which means making it a place where visitors stay because they find content and design that keeps them at your site.

Search programs are often generically referred to as search *engines* (and that terminology has been used so far in this chapter). To get listed by these programs, it's helpful to understand that, technically speaking, search *engines* and search *directories* use different techniques to list your site. Search *directories* organize web sites into categories (such as "Mission Style Furniture Builders"). These search directories rely on humans cataloging sites and listing them. Figure 8-2 shows the directory tree at Yahoo! to *Business and Economy > Business to Business > Communications and Networking > Internet and World Wide Web > Web Site Designers > By Region > U.S. States > North Dakota >*, and lists web design firms in North Dakota.

Figure 8-2
Yahoo! is a
search directory.

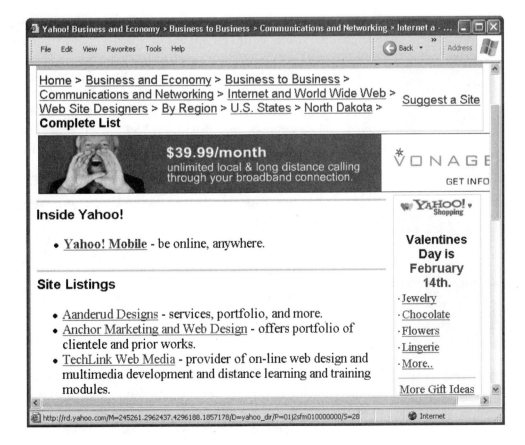

Search *engines* crawl the web, indexing the text on web pages. The index these programs create is used to look up matches when visitors type search criteria into a search engine box. Much of the art of being listed by search engines involves tuning the content of your pages so that visitors who search for terms related to your site *end up at your site.*

Finally, you have the option of paying an expert to improve your listing with search engines. These experts study the logic of the web crawler programs that index web pages, and they add content to your site that improves your listings. These experts engage in an ongoing guerrilla war with the developers of search engine programs—with the search engine programmers constantly updating their programs to evade "lures" set by firms that work to improve your site. While professionals who dedicate themselves to tricking search engines into providing better listings for a site can sometimes have some impact on site listings, there is much you can do on your own without paying a professional to get your site listed by search directories and search engines.

Step 1: Prepare Your Content for Search Engines

Search *engines* are probably the most widely used method to find web pages. Your goal is to have your site appear on the first page (usually the first ten listings) of results when a visitor searches for a phrase.

The first question to ask yourself is this: What phrase will folks use when they search for my site? If your site has a common name (such as Broadway Deli, for example), your goal might be to have your site appear in the first set of results when someone searches for "Broadway Deli." Or if you provide hot tub servicing in the greater Tucumcari, New Mexico, metro area, you might want your site to appear when someone searches for "hot tub servicing Tucumcari." It's important that you identify what phrase or phrases you expect folks to use when they search for your site. You'll use that phrase to adjust your web page content to attract search engine hits.

After you have identified the phrase that you think visitors will search for, you should *include that phrase in your home page* and in other pages in your site.

Use Your Page Titles to Attract Hits

You can improve your search engine results by using the phrase you want to target in search engines as your page *title*. For instance, if you're selling real estate in Golden Valley, Minnesota, and you want folks who search for "real estate in Golden Valley" to find your site, you can title your home page "Real Estate in Golden Valley." Defining page titles is explained for PageBuilder, FrontPage, and Dreamweaver in Chapters 4, 5, and 6 in this book.

Spiders (the programs used by search engines to index sites) are programmed to detect and *reject* sites that try to trick them with gratuitous or invisible use of phrases. Techniques such as repeating a phrase many times on your web page and formatting the text color so that the text is invisible on the page are considered a form of *spamming* (junk mailing) by search engine programs, and sites that use these techniques are often removed from search results lists. Don't try to fool search engines. But *do* use the phrase (or phrases) that you want search engines to index as much as possible in an appropriate way, integrated with your actual web page content.

Search engines don't like frames. If your web site uses frames, you'll probably want to remove them if search engine placement is important to you. As explained briefly in Chapters 5 and 6, when you generate frames, you embed your web pages inside a special web page that doesn't really include any content. It is the contentless, frameset page that is spidered by search engines, and they're not going to find anything to index.

Some but not all search engines will go on and locate content in your *framed* pages, but the pages they display in search result lists will be your embedded framed pages. Therefore, folks who find your pages in a search engine list will jump directly to an embedded frame, instead of the frameset page to which you intended them to go.

Expert web designers add content to what is called the NOFRAMES HTML tag to work around this problem, but even with that technique, frames make it less likely that your web pages will be indexed by a search engine.

Step 2: Check Your Keywords and Description Tags

After you've tweaked your web page content with search engines in mind, you can further improve your odds for being listed by adding keywords to your pages. You can control the description that appears for your site in a search engine by adding a description to your pages.

Some search engines provide a limited amount of spell-checking so that a visitor who searches for "buld your own web site" *might* see a list of matches for "*build* your own web site." But these correction features work only some of the time. Therefore, you'll want to anticipate different ways a visitor might spell the phrase or word you are targeting. For instance, if you provide hiking tours of Portugal, you might list both "Portuguese hiking tours" and "*Portugese* hiking tours" as keywords. In addition, anticipate different ways visitors might try to find you in a search engine.

The process of assigning keywords is different in PageBuilder, FrontPage, and Dreamweaver. Use the following instructions to add keywords to as many pages as you wish using your page design program.

In PageBuilder, assign keywords to an open page by choosing Format | Page Properties. Enter keyword phrases, separated by commas, in the Keywords box in the Page Properties dialog box, as shown in Figure 8-3. Then click OK.

Figure 8-3
Adding a list of
keywords and
a description to a
page in PageBuilder

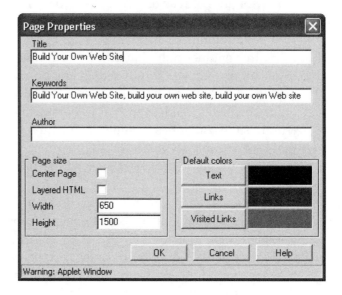

In FrontPage, you assign keywords to an open page by selecting File | Properties, and then clicking the Custom tab in the Page Properties dialog box. Click the Add button in the User Variables area of the Custom tab. In the Name area of the User Meta Variable dialog box, type **keywords**. In the Value area, type phrases, separated by commas, as shown next. Then click OK until all dialog boxes are closed.

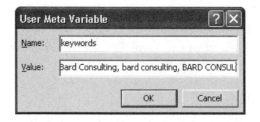

You can assign keywords to an open page in Dreamweaver by choosing Insert I Head Tags I Keywords. Enter keyword phrases separated by commas in the dialog box, and then click OK. When you save your page, the keywords are added. Figure 8-4 shows keywords being assigned in Dreamweaver.

Figure 8-4
Defining keywords
in Dreamweaver

The most important page for keywords and a description is your home page, but it is also helpful to assign keywords and a description to all the pages in your site.

Step 3: Submit Your Site to Google

The world of search engines is constantly evolving, but at this writing Google has established itself as the most popular based on its ability to produce accurate, useful search results. Many portals, including Netscape, Yahoo!, and AOL use the Google search engine to produce search results.

Before you submit your site to any search engine, you'll want to be sure that your content is *ready* to be indexed. Make sure you've completed Steps 1 and 2 in this chapter before you tell Google to go through your site and index it.

Google's search engine places a high priority on how many links lead to your site from other locations on the Internet. However, Google cautions against joining link exchanges and insists they will not improve your listing.

Once your site is ready, you can submit it to Google for spidering. Do that by going to *www.google.com/addurl.html* and entering your URL, as shown in Figure 8-5.

Figure 8-5
Registering your
site with Google

You can resubmit your site to Google without being penalized. You might want to do that if your page description or content changes significantly. Google also offers advertising, but advertised sites are listed separately from search results, and advertising does not affect your site's ranking at Google. One of the reasons Google has developed a reputation as the most useful search engine is that it makes a clear distinction between advertised sites and search engine results.

Step 4: Submit Your Site to Inktomi

The Inktomi search engine is less well known than Google, but among the portals that utilize it is Microsoft—which means that if someone types a word or phrase into the address line of Internet Explorer, the Inktomi search engine will look for that phrase. For this reason alone, a good listing from Inktomi is important.

To submit your site to Inktomi, go to Microsoft's Submit It service, at *http://submitit.bcentral.com/msnsubmit.htm*, and enter your URL and e-mail address, as shown in Figure 8-6. Inktomi respiders registered sites once a month.

Figure 8-6
Submitting your
site to Inktomi

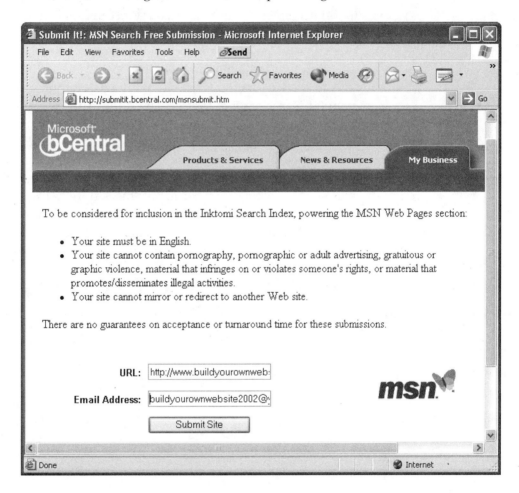

The Inktomi registration site includes links to a paid search engine registration site maintained by Submit It. The Submit It services does guarantee listings. Submit It and other pay-for-placement search programs charge either a fixed rate or sometimes charge per click to your site from search lists.

Step 5: Submit Your Site to Multiple Search Engines with Add Me

While Google and Inktomi are currently the most widely used search engines, dozens of other search engines are used as well. Registering your site with these search engines can be rather tedious, but you can find web sites that will do that work for you. These sites generally offer a free deal that allows you to register your site with a dozen or so search engines, and they offer pay deals that register your site with hundreds of search engines.

The Add Me site (*www.addme.com*) will register your site with many of the most popular search engines for free. The AddMe pay service registers your site with more search engines.

To use the Add Me service, go to *www.addme.com* and click the Free Search Engine Submission link. Follow additional links as necessary to get to the free search engine submission page. Add Me asks that you copy and paste HTML into your site promoting its service, but this is optional.

You'll be prompted to fill out a form with information about you and your site. After you submit that form, the Add Me site will assist you in submitting the information you gave to several search engines, as shown in Figure 8-7.

Figure 8-7
Submitting your site to a search engine using Add Me

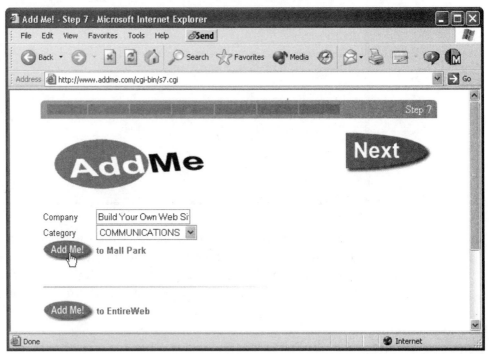

After using Add Me to submit your site to a search engine, you'll need to use the Back button in your browser to return to Add Me for assistance in adding your site to additional search engines.

Step 6: Submit Your Site to Yahoo!

Google, Inktomi, and other search engines spider your site and index it automatically. On the other hand, web *directories* such as Yahoo! or Open Directory list sites by categories and subcategories. To get listed in a web directory, you have to nominate your site for listing in a specific category. The administrators will review your site and decide whether or not to include you. Yahoo! charges (currently about $300) to review submissions for listing in a directory. However, noncommercial sites can be listed for free.

The easiest way to submit your site to a category at Yahoo! is to first navigate to that folder and then add your site. Start by locating the Web Site Directory section of the Yahoo! home page (at *www.yahoo.com*). Find a category link that encompasses the category you want your site listed at. You can either select a category by content (such as "Business and Economy" or "Health"), or you can use the Regional link to navigate to your region and list your site. Or you can do both. For example, a real estate consulting firm located on the Antarctic island of Kerguelen could be listed regionally by navigating to Regional | Countries | France | Overseas Territories | French Southern and Antarctic Lands | Islands | Kerguelen. Once you've navigated to the regional category you want to be listed at, click the Suggest A Site link on that page. If you are listing a noncommercial site, Yahoo! will offer you the option of paying to evaluate your submission within seven days or allowing you to submit a site for free with no guarantee as to how long it will take to review your submission. Select the paid option, or to submit your site for free, click the Standard Consideration button if available for your site content. If you are submitting a commercial site, you'll have to provide billing information for the Business Express Plan.

Before you submit your site, you'll be asked to confirm that you're at the category (either content or regional category) that you wish to be listed at, as shown in Figure 8-8. Click Confirm (or, if you're not happy with the listed category, go back to the Yahoo! home page and follow links to a better category).

Figure 8-8
Choosing a category
at the Yahoo!
directory to which
you want to submit
your site

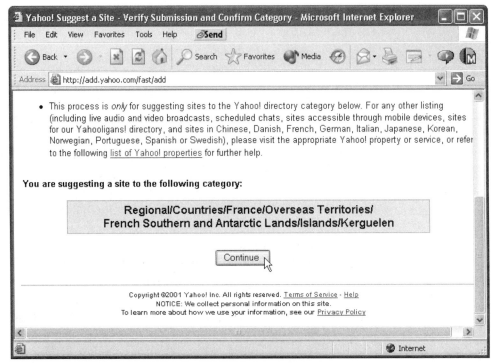

The final step is to fill out information on your site and submit that for review. Yahoo! will quickly verify that you've submitted a valid URL and promise to review your site for possible inclusion in its directory.

Step 7: Track Your Hits to Build Traffic

Once you've submitted your site to search engines, and you have developed plans to promote your site through mailings, press releases, e-mailings, and so on, you'll want to track hits to your site to evaluate the effectiveness of your site promotion plans. For instance, if you launch an ad campaign promoting your site, you'll want to compare hits before and after the ads run. If you use a pay-to-list service for your site with a search engine, you'll want to study the effect of that listing on visits to your site.

Most web site providers include some form of tracking service that lists how many hits have been received by your site, or by pages at your site, over a set time period. At GeoCities, for example, click the Site Statistics link to access a variety of site visit reports. The Page Views Report for a selected page, for instance, shows when visitors came to that page. Figure 8-9 displays this report.

Figure 8-9
Using a Site Statistics
report to evaluate
when visitors came
to a web page

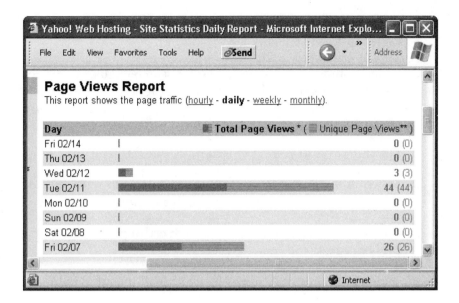

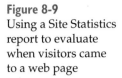

Need a Hit Counter?

If the reports available from your web host provider aren't sufficient, a number of free and commercial hit-log analyzers are available for download. You'll find them by searching for "hit counters."

Just as there are no easy tricks for losing weight or making money, there are no magic tricks or easy shortcuts for getting folks to come to your web site. You will build traffic at your web site by periodically improving your web content, submitting your web site to search engines, and studying what promotional activity generates hits to your site using statistics (usually) available from your site provider.

Use the following checklist to maintain your site's listing at search engines:

❏ Identify key phrases for your web site overall, and for individual pages, that you want to target for search engines.

❏ Assign an appropriate page title to every page using a phrase to attract search engines—whenever possible, use the exact wording of the phrase you've targeted for search engine listings.

❏ Add keyword lists to your pages that include the phrases you are targeting for search engines.

❏ Include phrases you are targeting for search engines in the content of your web pages, without using such tricks as repeated text or invisible text.

❏ Try to avoid frames.

❏ Develop links to your site from other sites.

❏ List your site with the main search engines and with selected search directories (such as Yahoo!, or search directories specific to your field).

❏ Promote your site offline through advertising, networking, mailings, press releases, and news coverage.

❏ Integrate promoting your web site into all the advertising and promotion activities of your company or organization.

❏ Study traffic to your web site to identify and utilize activity that improves traffic.

❏ Last but not least, include valuable content in your site to generate visitors and word-of-mouth promotion.

Chapter 9

Troubleshooting and Improving Your Site

In the unpredictable world of web site publishing, many things can go wrong to keep folks from being able to access your site. Your site might not upload at all, or it might upload, but some of your content might not be available online. Images can fail to appear, with web pages displaying ugly empty boxes instead of your logo, banner, or photo. In this chapter, you'll learn to troubleshoot many of the most common glitches that can occur while publishing your site.

Maintaining and improving your web site is an ongoing task. Keeping your site content fresh with new information and page design is essential if you are aiming to attract return visitors. Even if *your* site content doesn't change, you'll still want to keep your site updated by making sure links to *other* sites remain valid. As you get more experienced at web design, and your skills improve, you'll want to enhance the appearance and usability of your site. The second part of this chapter provides techniques and resources for ongoing site improvement.

Troubleshooting

You've designed and published your site, but it's not working! First of all, stay calm. Every web designer has gone through this experience—and more than once or twice! In the complex process of creating and uploading a web site, there are a lot of glitches that can arise. The following sections of this chapter will help you diagnose and fix those error messages, bad links, missing pictures, or slow pages that are driving you nuts.

Your Site Isn't Online

After you create your web site and upload it to your web server, you'll want to navigate to your site in your web browser and *make sure* the site is online. If your site doesn't appear online, that means something went wrong during the process of uploading your content from your local computer to your remote server. That problem might be on your end—either with the login information you defined for your site or with the Internet connection at your local computer. Or the problem might be at the server end—the web host administrator might not have properly assigned you access to your site. Before you call (or e-mail) your site administrator, you'll want to do some troubleshooting at your end first.

Both FrontPage and Dreamweaver have error tracking tools that will warn you if they are unable to upload your content to the server. Pages saved in GeoCities PageBuilder are automatically saved at the server, but if the connection to the server is corrupted—either because of a problem at the GeoCities server or a problem with your Internet connection—PageBuilder will not save your page at all.

Save Your Work

If any web design program crashes—and they do crash from time to time—you'll lose any work you've done on your page since you last saved your work. Be sure to save your work fairly frequently when you are editing web pages in PageBuilder, FrontPage, or Dreamweaver.

The process of tracking down the problem with your server connection is somewhat different for PageBuilder on the one hand, and FrontPage or Dreamweaver on the other. In PageBuilder, you do all your page editing *directly on the server*, so if the work is not appearing on your web site, the whole PageBuilder connection is corrupted. GeoCities servers are relatively reliable, but at times, too much traffic can cause disruptions in connectivity. The only "solution" is to log out of PageBuilder and reconnect.

In FrontPage and Dreamweaver, you generally build your site on your local computer and then upload it to the server. If you receive an error message during the upload process, it probably means that the information you supplied when you defined your web site is not meshing with the login information required by your web host provider. To track down the problem, get out (or request another copy of) the login information provided by your web host. Make sure that information includes the login name, password, and (for Dreamweaver users) the FTP address. Some web hosts require other information, so make sure you ask whether any other details are required for logging in.

Then check your site definition settings to make sure you entered the correct login info.

In FrontPage, the process of logging into a site is somewhat simplified because your server needs to have special programs called FrontPage Extensions that facilitate the connection between your computer and your server. To connect to a site in FrontPage, you need to know only your site's URL, your user name, and your password. To verify that you have the correct information, choose File | Open Web. In the Open Web dialog box, enter your site's full URL in the Web Name box and click Open. The dialog box shown next opens and prompts you for a User Name and Password. Reenter this information, as shown here:

In Dreamweaver, choose Site | Edit Sites to open the Edit Sites dialog box. If you have more than one site, choose the site you are working on from the list in the dialog box, and click Edit. Choose the Advanced tab in the Site Definition dialog box (if you are using Dreamweaver MX). In the HTTP Address box in the Local

Info category, make sure your URL is entered correctly—this is the web address (such as *http://www.buildyourownwebsite.us*). Select the Remote Info category and double-check to make sure the information you entered in the Access drop-down list (almost always "FTP"), the FTP Host box, the Login, and the Password are correct. Figure 9-1 shows the Advanced tab's Remote Info category of the Site Definition dialog box, with FTP host, login, and password reentered.

Figure 9-1
Double-check! If your connection is not working, reenter login info in Dreamweaver.

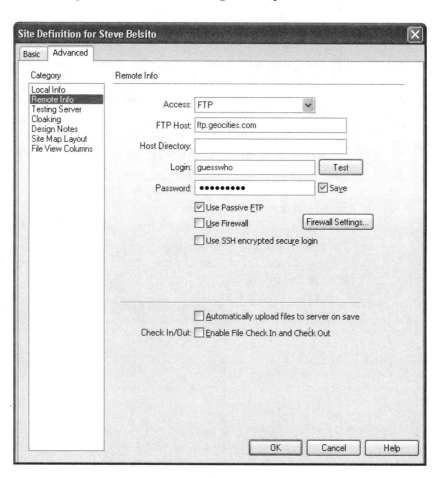

TIPS OF
THE TRADE

Use Passive FTP

As an additional troubleshooting trick, it never hurts to check the Use Passive FTP checkbox in the Site Definition dialog box. Passive FTP is a form or file transfer that originates the connection to the server from your computer, as opposed to initiating the connection from the server. Passive FTP is most useful for situations in which your local firewall might prevent active FTP from working correctly.

After you have double-checked all your login info, click the Test button (shown here in the left margin) in the Dreamweaver MX Site Definition dialog box. If your connection is fixed, you'll see a dialog box saying "Macromedia Dreamweaver MX connected to your Web server successfully." Click OK and then Done to exit the Site Definition dialog box. If you are using an older version of Dreamweaver that didn't provide the Test button in the Site Definition dialog box, click the Connect icon. Either your site will now connect, or you have a bigger problem. Once you've made sure you have the proper connection information, it's time to contact your web host administrator and ask him or her to track down the problem.

HEADS UP!

Are You Behind a Firewall?

If you are unable to connect to your server, one possible problem could be the interference of firewall software. Firewall software restricts what information can flow into and out of a local network. If your computer is behind a firewall, you'll need to ask your network administrator for firewall settings to enable you to upload and download to and from your site. Without these settings, you can't access your site.

In Dreamweaver, you (or better yet, your network administrator) can enter firewall settings by clicking the Firewall button in the Site Definition dialog box. In Dreamweaver, choose Site | Edit Site, and select your site from the list; then click the Edit button. Select the Advanced tab in the Site Definition dialog box (in MX only). Click the Remote Info category, and click the Use Firewall checkbox; then click Firewall Settings and enter information provided by your network administrator.

In FrontPage or PageBuilder, you'll need to have your site administrator assign you permission to upload and download content for your site.

To summarize, if you can't upload your site to your remote server, you've either entered the wrong settings in FrontPage or Dreamweaver, or your site administrator hasn't yet properly configured your remote site to allow you access. Since logging into your Yahoo! Mail account accesses your remote PageBuilder site, the only challenge to connecting to your PageBuilder server is to log in to your e-mail account.

Images Are Missing

Technically speaking, images that you embed in a web page are actually *linked* to that page. If the link you defined to an embedded image is broken, the page will display with an "X" and a blank box where the image should appear, as shown in Figure 9-2.

Figure 9-2
A corrupted link to an image is preventing the image from displaying—only the Alt text shows in the image box.

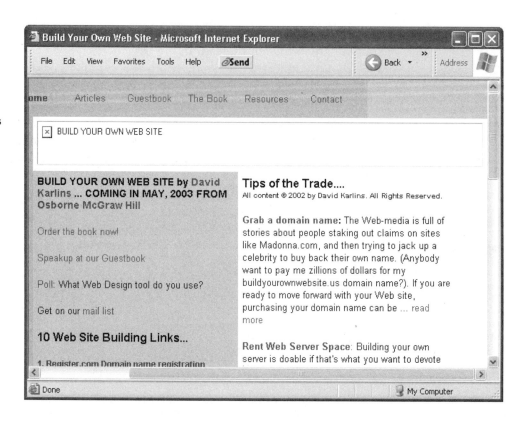

TIPS OF THE TRADE

Use Alt Tags

The corrupted image in Figure 9-2 displays text ("BUILD YOUR OWN WEB SITE" because an Alt tag was assigned to the image. In Dreamweaver, enter text in the Alt box of the Properties Inspector for a selected image. In FrontPage, type text in the Text box in the Picture Properties dialog box. In PageBuilder, enter text in the Screen Tip box of the Select Picture dialog box when you insert an image.

Image links can become corrupted when images are renamed or moved. Or sometimes images are not uploaded to the server. If your images aren't showing up in your pages, simply reinsert the image. PageBuilder, FrontPage, and

Dreamweaver will all restore corrupted image links if you reinsert the image on the page, save the page, and (when using Dreamweaver) upload (Put) the page to your server.

Yet another possibility is that the image is linked correctly and uploaded OK, but the image file itself is either corrupted (messed up) or is in a file format that isn't supported by web browsers (such as TIFF or BMP). In this situation, the image file itself must be repaired or saved to a web-compatible format (JPEG, GIF, or PNG).

Internal Links Don't Work

Links within your site can become corrupted if you rename a web page, if you move a web page to a different folder in your site, or if the target web page doesn't properly upload to your server.

As with broken picture links, the best way to restore a broken link is simply to redefine it using your web authoring software. (Refer back to Chapters 4, 5, and 6 for instructions on how to do this in PageBuilder, FrontPage, and Dreamweaver, respectively.) After you redefine links, upload *both* the page that has the link *and* the page that is the target of the link.

Your Site Is Too Slow

One of the most annoying impediments to folks visiting your site is pages that take too long to download. Generally speaking, formatted text downloads quickly. Images and media files can slow down your site.

As emphasized in Chapter 3, it's important that images be reduced in size *before* you start placing them on your web page. A large image that you reduce in size in Dreamweaver or PageBuilder will retain the original file size! (Only FrontPage allows you to reduce file size when you downsize an image.) Programs such as Adobe PhotoShop and Adobe Illustrator list download times for images, and users of those programs can reduce image size and quality to speed up download time. Tiled background images also take time to download, and they slow down your pages. Consider a solid color background instead of a tiling image to speed up your site.

If large images are important to your site content, consider using *thumbnails*—small versions of the image on your page. Thumbnail images can be linked to a fill-sized version of the image. Visitors who click a thumbnail are making a decision to wait a little while to see a full-sized image, but other visitors don't need to wait for large image files to download. Figure 9-3 shows a page that utilizes thumbnails to open larger images.

Figure 9-3
Each of these images is a link that opens a larger image.

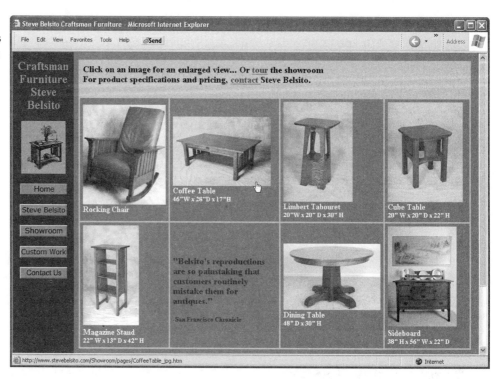

TIPS OF THE TRADE

Speed Up Page Downloading by Reusing Images

Images that are reused in a web site have to download only once. After that, they remain in the *cache* (temporary) memory on your computer. Whenever possible, reuse an image on several pages in your site, rather than forcing visitors to download new image files. For example, you can use the same navigation icons on each page, use the same page banner artwork, or use the same photo on several pages.

Programs like Photoshop and Illustrator also allow you to add *interlacing* to GIF images, and *progressive display* to JPEGs. These features make the wait more pleasant as images download by having the image "fade in" as opposed to appearing line by line, from top to bottom. Ask your graphic designer to use progressive display or interlacing in your web images.

Background sound files can increase page download time tremendously, and they are rarely worth the wait. If your page downloads too slowly, get rid of page background sounds.

Maintaining and Improving Your Site

The Internet is a *now* medium, and visitors to your site will expect current material, updated links *that work*, and periodic refreshing of your site design. Keeping your web site fresh and working smoothly is an ongoing process, and should be built into your plan for your web site.

Test Your Links

A web site can easily have dozens, hundreds, or even thousands of links. You don't want to have to check them all the time to make sure they're still working! FrontPage and Dreamweaver include link-checking features, but you can also find free link-checking tools on the web.

In Dreamweaver MX, expand the Site panel (or press F7 to switch to the Site window in Dreamweaver 4). Then choose Site | Check Links Sitewide to generate a report with the status of all links. The Dreamweaver report shown in Figure 9-4 has identified a busted link to the *Banner.gif* file on the page *index.htm*.

Figure 9-4
Dreamweaver will test for corrupted links to pages or images.

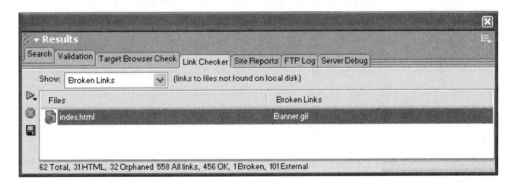

In FrontPage, choose View | Reports | Problems | Broken Hyperlinks to generate a list of broken links. If you created your site with PageBuilder, Seventwentyfour (*www.seventwentyfour.com*) will test all the links at the first 500

pages of your site and send you a report listing broken links. This site currently offers a 30-day free trial, which you can take advantage of to troubleshoot the links at your site.

Keep Content Fresh

Web page content can get stale. Text reminding visitors that your "Special Offer Ends January 1, 1995!" is a sure sign your site content isn't fresh. Updating the content of a web site has to be integrated into the ongoing functioning of any organization or business.

How often you schedule site updates depends on the type of site you are designing. A theater company will want to have a current schedule online. A school will want the upcoming semester's course list available. A nonprofit will want to update its site to promote new projects and provide visitors with current staff contact information. Every site needs a plan to keep the site up-to-date.

Make Your Site Accessible

By some reports, 20 percent of the people surfing the web have physical problems that prevent them from fully utilizing web sites. Visitors with impaired sight obviously cannot see images. Visitors with epilepsy and similar disabilities must avoid strobing (flickering) animation. Visitors who cannot use a mouse must rely on their keyboard or voice to access and follow links.

The most important thing you can do to make your site accessible is to add Alt text to your images. The process of adding Alt text was described earlier in this chapter in the section "Images Are Missing." Chapters 4, 5, and 6 include instructions for adding Alt text in PageBuilder (use the instructions for adding Screen Tips), in FrontPage, and in Dreamweaver.

Sight-impaired visitors surf the web using special *reader* software that reads web page content to them out loud. This reader software reads Alt text for an image, allowing sightless visitors to hear the content of the image.

The most accessible links for disabled visitors are text links. Image links, navigation icons that require the Flash player and other forms of navigation, are less accessible. At the least, every page should have text links available for site navigation.

Dreamweaver MX has features that allow page designers to add special HTML code that is interpreted by web readers. To access these features, choose

Edit | Preferences (Dreamweaver | Preferences in Mac OSX), and select the Accessibility Category. Select all the checkboxes in the Show Attributes When Inserting section of the dialog box, as shown in Figure 9-5, and click OK.

Figure 9-5
Selecting all attributes

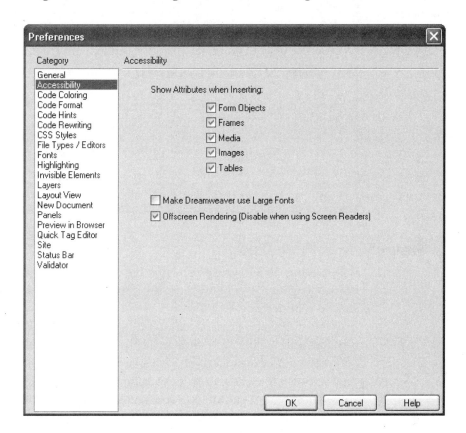

Handicapped accessibility is sometimes referred to as *508 Compliance*, in ref erence to a section of U.S. federal law mandating that sites built under contract to U.S. government agencies meet standards for accessibility. To test your site for 508 Compliance, go to *http://bobby.watchfire.com* and enter your site in the form box. Click the 508 Compliance button and then click Submit to test your site. Bobby will produce a report evaluating your site for 508 Compliance and identify areas of noncompliance. In Figure 9-6, the web page is missing an Alt tag (Alt text) for an image.

Figure 9-6
Busted—this page
needs Alt text
assigned to an
image before it
is considered
accessible.

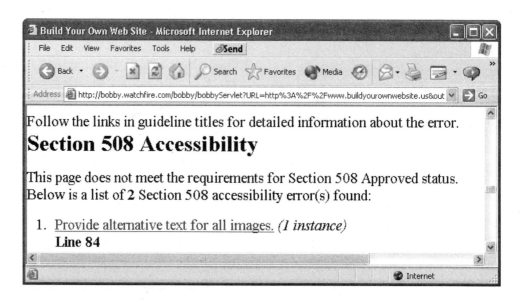

Simplify Your Page Design

Volumes have been written on effective web page design, many offering conflicting advice. But the general consensus among professional page designers is that simple is better.

You want web page content to be clear and readable. You want images to be minimal and small. Studies repeatedly show that while web designers love to add media and graphics, web visitors want to be able to find content easily, and they appreciate clean, no-frills web pages.

Make sure that visitors to your pages can quickly and easily navigate around your site with well-placed links. Ask yourself the following questions: What other pages do you want visitors to be able to access from your site? Are links to those pages easy to find? Further, you can improve your site design by pretending that you are a visitor to your own site. Is the content clear? Are links easy to find? Are pages that should be linked to each other actually linked? Make notes as you test your site, and add links as needed.

For no-nonsense advice on designing easy-to-navigate web pages, visit Jacob Nielson's Useit site—*www.useit.com/*. For humorous and helpful page design tips, visit *www.webpagesthatsuck.com*.

Periodically, visit sites with content or themes similar to yours, and note design approaches you want to "borrow" for your own site.

Improve Your Site's Color Scheme

As your site design skills mature, you'll pay more attention to establishing a coherent and attractive color scheme across your site. A uniform color scheme gives your site consistency, and makes visitors think the pages they visit are all part of a larger site.

You want to restrict your color scheme to as few colors as possible to give your site an uncluttered, consistent theme. You'll need to use three colors for links. By default, unvisited links are blue, visited links are purple, and active links (those being clicked) are red. You can choose a color for your page backgrounds and a color for your default text color; that may use up five colors. If you allow for three more colors for graphic elements (such as logos or page banners), you can keep your color scheme constrained to a total of eight colors.

To get your juices flowing, visit Lynda Weinman's inspiration page at *www.lynda.com/resources/inspiration/* and click the Color link.

Use Visitor Feedback

A link for visitor feedback is one of the most valuable elements on your web pages. Visitor feedback is a way of getting *free* advice and error checking for your site. Feedback also provides a way of learning what your visitors think of your site—and changes they'd like to see.

You can get all this by simply placing a "feedback" link on your web pages. That link can allow visitors to send you e-mail at your e-mail address.

As you "finish" your web site, you simultaneously enter the never-ending phase of testing, fixing, updating, and improving your site. Use the following table to schedule and manage ongoing site care and repair.

Item	How to Check	✓
Are links (including images) working?	Run test in FrontPage or Dreamweaver or use *www.seventwentyfour.com*.	❑
Are pages loading too slowly?	Test site using a 28.8K dialup connection.	❑
Is site content fresh?	Schedule periodic content updating.	❑

Item	How to Check	✓
Is site fully accessible?	Test at *http://bobby.watchfire.com.*	❑
Is page design effective?	Compare to similar sites, check advice at *www.useit.com* and *www.webpagesthatsuck.com.*	❑
Is color scheme uniform and effective?	Go to *www.lynda.com/resources/inspiration* for insights.	❑
Are you collecting visitor feedback?	Include an e-mail link for visitors to provide suggestions, and check that e-mail account regularly.	❑

Index

INTERNATIONAL CONTACT INFORMATION

AUSTRALIA
McGraw-Hill Book Company Australia Pty. Ltd.
TEL +61-2-9900-1800
FAX +61-2-9878-8881
http://www.mcgraw-hill.com.au
books-it_sydney@mcgraw-hill.com

CANADA
McGraw-Hill Ryerson Ltd.
TEL +905-430-5000
FAX +905-430-5020
http://www.mcgraw-hill.ca

GREECE, MIDDLE EAST, & AFRICA
(Excluding South Africa)
McGraw-Hill Hellas
TEL +30-210-6560-990
TEL +30-210-6560-993
TEL +30-210-6560-994
FAX +30-210-6545-525

MEXICO (Also serving Latin America)
McGraw-Hill Interamericana Editores S.A. de C.V.
TEL +525-117-1583
FAX +525-117-1589
http://www.mcgraw-hill.com.mx
fernando_castellanos@mcgraw-hill.com

SINGAPORE (Serving Asia)
McGraw-Hill Book Company
TEL +65-6863-1580
FAX +65-6862-3354
http://www.mcgraw-hill.com.sg
mghasia@mcgraw-hill.com

SOUTH AFRICA
McGraw-Hill South Africa
TEL +27-11-622-7512
FAX +27-11-622-9045
robyn_swanepoel@mcgraw-hill.com

SPAIN
McGraw-Hill/Interamericana de España, S.A.U.
TEL +34-91-180-3000
FAX +34-91-372-8513
http://www.mcgraw-hill.es
professional@mcgraw-hill.es

UNITED KINGDOM, NORTHERN,
EASTERN, & CENTRAL EUROPE
McGraw-Hill Education Europe
TEL +44-1-628-502500
FAX +44-1-628-770224
http://www.mcgraw-hill.co.uk
computing_europe@mcgraw-hill.com

ALL OTHER INQUIRIES Contact:
McGraw-Hill/Osborne
TEL +1-510-596-6600
FAX +1-510-596-7600
http://www.osborne.com
omg_international@mcgraw-hill.com